Will to Fight of Private Military Actors

Applying Cognitive Maneuver to Russian
Private Forces

MOLLY DUNIGAN AND ANTHONY ATLER

 ARROYO CENTER

For more information on this publication, visit **www.rand.org/t/RRA355-1**.

About RAND

The RAND Corporation is a research organization that develops solutions to public policy challenges to help make communities throughout the world safer and more secure, healthier and more prosperous. RAND is nonprofit, nonpartisan, and committed to the public interest. To learn more about RAND, visit www.rand.org.

Research Integrity

Our mission to help improve policy and decisionmaking through research and analysis is enabled through our core values of quality and objectivity and our unwavering commitment to the highest level of integrity and ethical behavior. To help ensure our research and analysis are rigorous, objective, and nonpartisan, we subject our research publications to a robust and exacting quality-assurance process; avoid both the appearance and reality of financial and other conflicts of interest through staff training, project screening, and a policy of mandatory disclosure; and pursue transparency in our research engagements through our commitment to the open publication of our research findings and recommendations, disclosure of the source of funding of published research, and policies to ensure intellectual independence. For more information, visit www.rand.org/about/research-integrity.

RAND's publications do not necessarily reflect the opinions of its research clients and sponsors.

Library of Congress Cataloging-in-Publication Data is available for this publication.

ISBN: 978-1-9774-0647-7

Cover: Undated photo purporting to show Wagner Group contractors, likely in Syria, released by the Security Service of Ukraine. Background photo by Tejasvi Ganjoo/Unsplash.

Preface

This report documents research and analysis conducted as part of a project entitled *Will to Fight in Overseas Contingencies: Breaking Adversaries Through Cognitive Maneuver,* sponsored by U.S. Army Special Operations Command. The purpose of the larger project was to analyze the will to fight of a selected set of adversary forces in named overseas contingencies, identify strengths and vulnerabilities that might be exploited, and develop a game or simulation to explore cognitive maneuver options to break adversaries' will to fight.

This research was conducted within RAND Arroyo Center's Strategy, Doctrine, and Resources Program. RAND Arroyo Center, part of the RAND Corporation, is a federally funded research and development center (FFRDC) sponsored by the United States Army.

RAND operates under a "Federal-Wide Assurance" (FWA00003425) and complies with the *Code of Federal Regulations for the Protection of Human Subjects Under United States Law* (45 CFR 46), also known as "the Common Rule," as well as with the implementation guidance set forth in DoD Instruction 3216.02. As applicable, this compliance includes reviews and approvals by RAND's Institutional Review Board (the Human Subjects Protection Committee) and by the U.S. Army. The views of sources utilized in this study are solely their own and do not represent the official policy or position of DoD or the U.S. Government.

Contents

Figures and Tables

Summary

The research reported here was completed in July 2020, followed by security review by the sponsor and the U.S. Army Office of the Chief of Public Affairs, with final sign-off in June 2023.

The work therefore predates Russia's 2022 invasion of Ukraine, and largely omits consideration of Russian private military forces in the war in Ukraine. Nonetheless, as of June 2023, this analysis remains relevant to an in-depth, long-term understanding of Russian private military actors and their will to fight.

In Syria, Ukraine, several African countries, and other conflict hotspots around the globe, private contractors operating on behalf of, yet are ostensibly separate from, the Russian state. These developments have prompted questions and concern within military and policy circles in light of the current U.S. focus on great power competition with Russia and China,[1] and the extent to which Russia has been exerting malign influence in conflicts worldwide through the use of proxy forces, including private military actors. The Army, the joint force, and U.S. allies and partners require a better understanding of the role that these Russian-hired private military actors play in conflicts, how to address their presence in operational planning, and the implications for U.S. policy with regard to Russia. The United States and its allies may be able to counter these forces through *cogni-*

---

[1] U.S. Department of Defense, *Summary of the 2018 National Defense Strategy of the United States of America: Sharpening the American Military's Competitive Edge*, January 19, 2018.

tive maneuver. U.S. Army Special Operations Command (USASOC) recognizes that the best way to win wars may be to use force in the multidomain context to achieve cognitive objectives—to change minds, to change behaviors, to win.[2]

With a specific focus on the case of Russian private military activity in Syria between 2015 and 2019, the purpose of this report is to apply a model developed at RAND to explore adversaries' "will to fight" to an analysis of (1) what motivates and demotivates Russian private military contractors in Syria and the companies that hire them to fight; (2) what influences the Russian government's decisions about whether and how to utilize private military actors in Syria; and (3) how USASOC and other U.S. government entities can leverage cognitive maneuver to counter these actors.[3] To that end, this report addresses the following research questions:

1. Who are the relevant actors in the Russian private military sphere to consider when assessing Russian private forces' will to fight?
2. What factors are most relevant to Russian private military actors' will to fight?
3. How do Russian private military actors compare with their current and historical Western counterparts, and what lessons can be drawn from these comparative cases to inform U.S. opportunities to counter adversary-employed private military actors?

---

[2]   U.S. Army Special Operations Command, *Expanding Maneuver in the Early 21st Century Security Environment*, January 12, 2017; Allison Astorino-Courtois, ed., *A Cognitive Capabilities Agenda: A Multi-Step Approach for Closing DoD's Cognitive Capability Gap*, Washington, D.C.: Joint Staff, Strategic Multi-Layer Assessment Office, October 2017; Patricia DeGennaro, "The Power of Cognitive Maneuver: Don't Underestimate Its Value," *Small Wars Journal*, September 19, 2017.

[3]   For more on the underlying model, see Ben Connable, Michael J. McNerney, William Marcellino, Aaron Frank, Henry Hargrove, Marek N. Posard, S. Rebecca Zimmerman, Natasha Lander, Jasen J. Castillo, and James Sladden, *Will to Fight: Analyzing, Modeling, and Simulating the Will to Fight of Military Units*, Santa Monica, Calif.: RAND Corporation, RR-2341-A, 2018.

We employed a multimethod qualitative approach to address these questions, including a media analysis, a literature review, conversations with subject-matter experts, and a limited number of semistructured interviews with foreign military personnel who had operational experience with Russian private military actors. Finally, we performed selective case-study analyses of analogous instances of private military contractor employment to derive lessons learned and identify particular individual, corporate, and client-state and societal factors that may make private military forces vulnerable to cognitive maneuver and attendant declines in their will to fight.

This topic is important for several reasons. First, all U.S. government agencies and military services should be concerned about Russia's increasing use of private military actors worldwide. These deployments allow Russia to expand its military footprint while maintaining plausible deniability in major combat operations and competition short of armed conflict. To effectively engage on this topic, the U.S. Army needs to be well informed regarding Russian private military actors' characteristics, activities, motives, and vulnerabilities. Second, USASOC forces have a potentially unique role to play in implementing U.S. military strategy vis-à-vis private military actors, especially in competition short of armed conflict, because of their positions in theaters of interest and their particular skill sets. Indeed, Army psychological operations, civil affairs, and special operations personnel are likely to be called upon to pursue cognitive maneuver activities, such as messaging and information operations, to stymie Russian private military activity. Therefore, it is critical for the U.S. Army and USASOC-aligned forces to develop a foundational understanding of Russian private military actors and their activities, as well as potential methods for exploiting their vulnerabilities.

Who Are the Relevant Actors in the Russian Private Military Sphere?

Russia has a long history of relying on former military personnel and intelligence specialists to reinforce its national interests in areas that are most critical to the state's leading exports: energy and arms. Most modern Russian private military actors can trace their lineage back to Alpha Group and its sister unit, Vympel (also known as Vega Group), counterterrorism and counterespionage units formed under the auspices of the KGB's development courses for officers following the dissolution of the Soviet Union. Alpha Group and Vympel, in turn, have ties to World War II–era partisan warfare units and the creation of specialized irregular reconnaissance task forces in the 1950s.[4]

One of the most recent iterations of the Russian marketized force model is the Wagner Group, founded in 2014 by Dmitry Utkin, former commander of the Russian military intelligence directorate's (GRU's) Spetsnaz special forces units. That same year, Wagner contractors took part in the annexation of Crimea and fought in the Donbass conflict in eastern Ukraine. In fall 2015, when Moscow launched its military intervention in Syria, Wagner deployed more than 2,000 personnel to support the campaign; that number grew to 5,000 by 2017.[5] The Wagner Group has also reportedly operated in Sudan, the Central African Republic, Madagascar, Libya, Mozambique, Mali, and Venezuela. Russia's use of the Wagner Group as a paramilitary entity grew quickly and extensively during the war in Ukraine, and by 2023, the group was reportedly employing 50,000 fighters at one time on Ukrainian soil.[6]

Other Russian private military companies (PMCs) that have appeared, to varying extents, in traditional media and online social media reporting since 2001 include the following:

---

[4] Candace Rondeaux, *Decoding the Wagner Group: Analyzing the Role of Private Military Security Contractors in Russian Proxy Warfare*, Washington, D.C.: New America, November 7, 2019, pp. 25–26.

[5] Metin Gurcan, "Private Military Companies: Moscow's Other Army in Syria," Al-Monitor, November 30, 2017.

[6] Ryan Browne, "Top US General Warns Russia Using Mercenaries to Access Africa's Natural Resources," CNN, February 7, 2019; Tim Lister, Sebastian Shukla, and Clarissa Ward, "Putin's Private Army," CNN, August 2019; Jane Flanagan, "Mozambique Calls on Russian Firepower," *The Times*, October 2, 2019; Kimberly Marten, "Russia's Use of Semi-State Security Forces: The Case of the Wagner Group," *Post-Soviet Affairs*, Vol. 35, No. 3, 2019; "What Is Russia's Wagner Group of Mercenaries and Why Did It March on Moscow?" BBC News, June 26, 2023.

- Anti-Terror Orel
- Slavonic Corps
- Moran Security Group
- RSB Group
- E.N.O.T. Corps
- MAR
- DOBRANDR
- Turan
- Centre R
- ATK Group
- Tigr Top-Rent Security
- Cossacks
- Patriot.[7]

Media and scholarly writing, relying on a mix of hard evidence and anecdotal speculation, indicates that contractors working under the auspices of one or more of these companies have operated in Iraq, Afghanistan, Ukraine, Syria, Libya, Chechnya, Tajikistan, Yemen, Burundi, and earlier incarnations of the conflict in Ukraine—some as far back as the late 1990s.[8]

What Factors Are Most Relevant to Russian Private Military Actors' Will to Fight?

The will-to-fight model was developed to assess the will to fight of *military forces* and so could not be adopted wholesale to examine the motivations of private military actors. Our research identified six factors as particularly important for understanding the will to fight of private military actors (specifically, Russian private military actors). These

---

[7]   The industry's lack of transparency limits analysts' ability to track the existence and activities of Russian private military actors, though many have tried. See, for example, Marten, 2019 and Sergey Sukhankin, *"Continuing War by Other Means": The Case of Wagner, Russia's Premier Private Military Company in the Middle East*, Washington, D.C.: Jamestown Foundation, July 13, 2018b.

[8]   Browne, 2019; Lister, Shukla, and Ward, 2019; Flanagan, 2019; Marten, 2019.

factors are outlined in red in Figure S.1. Those outlined in gray were potentially relevant in determining private military actors' operational effectiveness, but we found that these factors were not decisive in motivating them to fight.

What Lessons Can Be Drawn from Comparative Cases to Counter Adversary-Employed Private Military Actors?

Applying the modified will-to-fight model led us to the following conclusions with regard to this population.

Identity

The individual identities of contractor personnel vary and may not align with the goals of the Russian state or PMC leadership goals in ordering the deployment. Therefore, the impact of identity on will to fight is variable. However, detailed analyses of private military contractors' individual identities provide insight into potential vulnerabilities regarding their will to fight.

Data limitations make it difficult to discern the relevant components of the identities of Russian private military actors operating in any given area, but in the Syrian conflict (between 2015 and 2019), we know that they were typically Eastern European, possibly (but not necessarily) patriotic, and most likely had military or intelligence background and skill sets that they sought to apply to lucrative work beyond the military.

Individual Well-Being

Challenges to individual well-being may decrease one's will to fight, as well as effective occupational functioning while performing tasks related to a contracted, military-relevant position in theater. Anecdotal reports indicate that some Russian contractors have returned home from Syrian deployments with posttraumatic stress disorder and physical and mental health problems that are likely to go unaddressed over the long term.

Figure S.1
Factors Relevant to Private Military Actors' Will to Fight

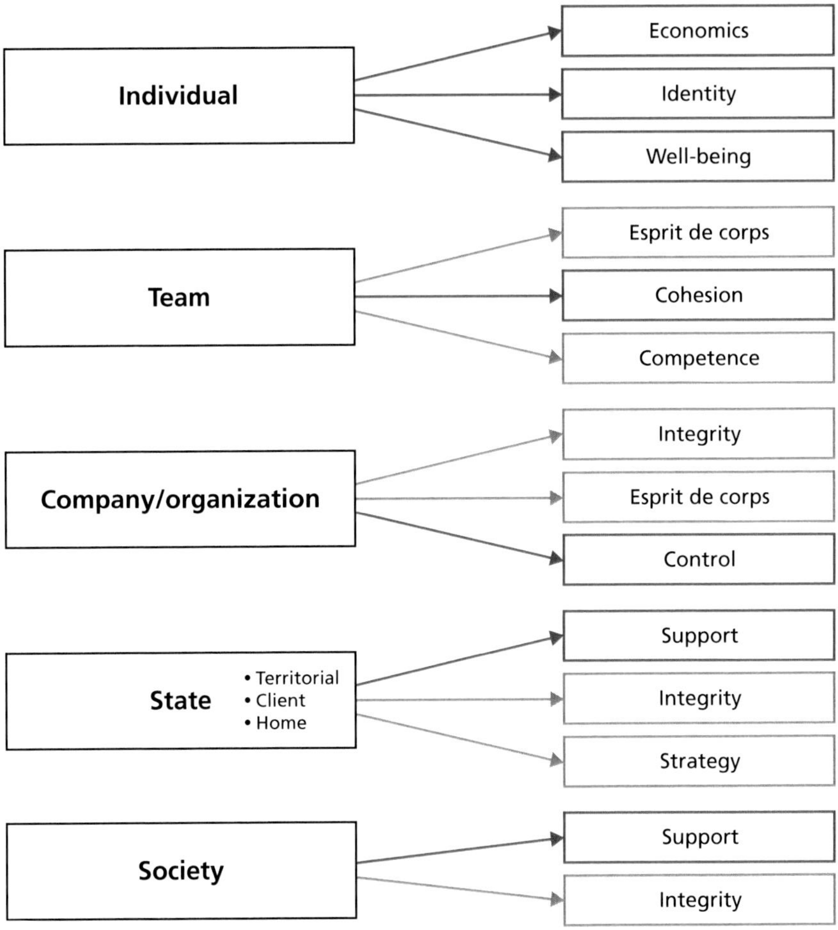

SOURCE: Identified factors draw on the military will-to-fight model described in Connable et al., 2018, with the exception of individual well-being, an addition suggested by this research.

NOTES: A red outline indicates a key factor that determines a Russian private military actor's will to fight: economic pressures, identity, individual well-being, unit cohesion, organizational control, and degree of support at the state and societal levels. The remaining factors (outlined in gray) are potentially relevant to the effectiveness of private military actors but were not decisive in motivating them to fight.

Economics

Economic factors in the military will-to-fight model can be associated with oneself or one's family and include several drivers that can directly affect an individual's will to fight: (1) the need for subsistence, (2) the desire for socioeconomic advancement, and (3) the motivation to earn money and improve quality of life.

Compiled data from media reports indicate that pay rates for Russian private military actors—even at the more senior operational levels—are significantly lower than for Western contractors who provide security services in theaters of conflict under the auspices of Western PMCs. However, the pay offered to contractors who work for Russian private military actors was significantly higher than the average monthly salary in Russia as of early 2020 and was, in some cases, higher than what U.S. prime contractors paid Eastern European nationals for their service in Iraq in the early and mid-2000s.

Cohesion

High levels of task cohesion between private military actors and their state military counterparts can increase military effectiveness by positively influencing will to fight at the team level. Notably, at least one currently active Russian PMC, the Wagner Group, appears to maintain a clear and well-developed command-and-control (C2) system within its own company formations, following a template drawn from the structure of the Russian armed forces. Such a structured C2 approach may assist in improving task cohesion between contractors and the allied military forces they deploy alongside, although co-deployment of military and private forces is typically quite challenging and can lead to coordination problems, friendly-fire issues, or outright violence.[9]

Control

The concept of control reflects the relationship between individual and higher-level factors. For example, individual will to fight may not be inherently strong, but unit- and organization-level coercion may be

---

[9]   Molly Dunigan, *Victory for Hire: Private Security Companies' Impact on Military Effectiveness*, Stanford University Press, 2011.

sufficiently strong that, on the surface, the will to fight of the entire unit or organization appears to be quite robust. Thus, will to fight may be vulnerable if individuals are targeted, but there is a risk such efforts will fail due to unit or organizational oversight.

The private military industry is illegal in Russia, and some speculate that this intentional illegality is a mechanism for Putin or the Russian Federal Security Service to control private military actors and ensure their loyalty. Other mechanisms of both unit and organizational control appear to include recruiting personnel with promises of lucrative and easy work, then holding their passports until their contract has been fulfilled.

Support

A lack of state or societal support can weaken will to fight. Russian private military actors and their Western counterparts have appeared over time to receive comparable levels of state support. For example, wounded contractors who work for Russian companies are treated in Russian hospitals and share training sites with Russian military bases. Yet, due to the industry's illegal status in Russia, state support wavers at times. Societal support is more tenuous, and it is the *absence* of societal awareness and hence support that seems to enable Russia's use of private military actors and thus may be a vulnerability in these forces' will to fight. Indeed, intentional obfuscation regarding contractor casualty counts has led to a dearth of Russian popular attention to the use of contractors, which equates to a public "nod" to these deployments.

The Best Options for Countering Adversary-Employed Private Military Actors in Syria and Beyond

We recommend that USASOC and the broader U.S. government pursue three lines of effort moving forward to exploit vulnerabilities associated with Russia's use of private military actors. Many of these recommendations center on messaging activities that are likely to be conducted by USASOC psychological operations forces; however, all

USASOC components should look for opportunities to exploit these vulnerabilities within their own mission sets.

Individual and Company/Organizational Levels: Exploit Vulnerabilities in the Recruitment and Retention of Promising Contractor Personnel

Analyses via the lenses of the *identity, economics, individual well-being,* and *control* factors provide insight into conceivably fruitful cognitive maneuver activities for USASOC to pursue at the individual and company/organizational levels. It appears that Russian contractor personnel tend to select this type of work for self-interested or clientelistic reasons and are often not treated well by the Russian government. Indeed, in some cases, it appears that they are victims of outright exploitation by the state or the companies they work for. These individuals may therefore be moderately vulnerable and their loyalties highly malleable. It follows that efforts to weaken their loyalty and commitment may prove fruitful.

Options for exploiting such vulnerabilities could include overt messaging efforts through social media and other venues to highlight the inequities in pay and living conditions between operational contractors on the ground and individuals higher in the ranks of the PMC corporate structure, or to highlight to the demographic of potential recruits the coercive nature of such contracts. Moreover, broad messaging of statistics regarding contractors' deployment-related physical and mental health and challenges acquiring long-term treatment for these problems could affect recruitment of both new and veteran contractors over time.

Team Level: Exploit and Deepen Potential Discord Between Contractor and Military Populations

Analyses via the lens of the *cohesion* factor—specifically, task cohesion—provide insight into potentially fruitful cognitive maneuver activities for USASOC to pursue at the team level. Western uses of PMCs have provided abundant examples of poor coordination and, at times, hostile or deadly interactions between contractors and supposedly allied military forces.[10] U.S. psychological operations and special operations forces could fruitfully explore methods of sowing disorder and resentment between Russian private military contractors and Russian military forces, both in high-tension combat operations and in everyday interactions outside of the conflict space, including domestically in Russia and Eurasia.

State and Societal Levels: Widely Disseminate Information About Contractors' Veteran Status and Contractor Casualties to the Russian Public

Analyses via the lens of the *support* factor provide insight into potentially fruitful cognitive maneuver activities for the U.S. government to pursue at the state and societal levels—possibly with support from USASOC. There is evidence that contractor casualties are significantly underreported in Russia and that contractors' families are prohibited from talking to the media if they hope to receive death compensation. In an effort to foster societal backlash within Russia against the Russian government's utilization of private military actors, U.S. forces should consider methods to broadly disseminate information about Russian involvement in foreign conflicts—including the use of Russian veterans in private military roles and their subsequent treatment—to the Russian public, as well as data on contractor casualties.

---

[10] Dunigan, 2011, Chapter 3; David Phinney, "Marines Jail Contractors in Iraq: Tension and Confusion Grow Amid the 'Fog of War,'" CorpWatch, June 7, 2005; Ariel Zilber, "Ex–Green Beret and Father-of-Four Who Worked as a Contractor for Lockheed Martin Dies After Being 'Pummeled into Unconsciousness by Two Marines During a Gym Altercation' While Working in Iraq," *Daily Mail*, January 8, 2019.

Acknowledgments

We gratefully acknowledge the assistance of a number of foreign military personnel who took the time to speak with us for the purposes of this study. Although we cannot name them publicly, we are indebted to them for their assistance. We thank Ben Connable and Michael McNerney for their deft leadership of the project for which we conducted this research and for their guidance on applying the will-to-fight model to this case. Jennifer Kavanagh and Stephen Watts provided valuable RAND management support. We also thank Deborah Avant at the University of Denver and Anika Binnendijk at RAND for their careful reviews of the report. The U.S. Army Special Operations Command G-9 directorate deserves special thanks for funding this research, and we would especially like to thank Brooke Tannehill for the guidance that he and his team provided over the course of our study.

Abbreviations

C2	command and control
DoD	U.S. Department of Defense
FSB	Russian Federal Security Service
GRU	Glavnoye Razvedyvatelnoye Upravleniye [Russian Intelligence Directorate]
KGB	Komitet Gosudarstvennoy Bezopasnosti [Committee for State Security]
LOGCAP	Logistics Civil Augmentation Program
PMC	private military company
PMSC	private military and security company
PSC	private security company
PTSD	posttraumatic stress disorder
TCN	third-country national
USASOC	U.S. Army Special Operations Command

CHAPTER ONE

Understanding the Will to Fight of Private Military Actors

The research reported here was completed in July 2020, followed by security review by the sponsor and the U.S. Army Office of the Chief of Public Affairs, with final sign-off in June 2023.

The work therefore predates Russia's 2022 invasion of Ukraine, and largely omits consideration of Russian private military forces in the war in Ukraine. Nonetheless, as of June 2023, this analysis remains relevant to an in-depth, long-term understanding of Russian private military actors and their will to fight.

In Ukraine, Syria, and other conflict hotspots around the globe, private contractors are operating on behalf of, yet are ostensibly separate from, the Russian state. Indeed, there is documentation that the Russian Wagner Group is or has recently been active in Ukraine, Syria, Sudan, the Central African Republic, Madagascar, Libya, Mozambique, Mali, and Venezuela.[1]

Russian private military actors appear to be somewhat unique in that they have a direct relationship with Russian state leadership, but they technically remain illegal under Russian law. Moreover, although Russian military force privatization has roots extending back to the end of the Cold War, the extent to which the Russian state employs

---

[1] Ryan Browne, "Top US General Warns Russia Using Mercenaries to Access Africa's Natural Resources," *CNN*, February 7, 2019; Tim Lister, Sebastian Shukla, and Clarissa Ward, 'Putin's Private Army," *CNN*, August 2019; Jane Flanagan, "Mozambique Calls on Russian Firepower," *The Times*, October 2, 2019.

private military actors has exploded in the past decade. These actors are increasingly thought to constitute a critical, planned component of Russia's military end strength for ground operations, and they are intrinsically tied to protecting and sustaining two of Russia's leading exports: energy and arms.[2]

Against the development of Russia's "new generation warfare" concept—which emphasizes the growing use of nonmilitary means in combination with military tools to achieve political ends—this increasing reliance on private actors for military functions around the globe is striking.[3] In the context of the current U.S. focus on great power competition with Russia and China,[4] and in light of the increasing extent to which Russia is exerting malign influence in proxy conflicts worldwide, the U.S. Army, joint force, and U.S. allies and partners need to consider and better understand these Russian-hired private military actors and how best to combat them. Indeed, given that private military actors are central to Russia's new generation model of warfare, an ability to erode or disrupt their effective use would deny the Russian government a critical tool in achieving its political and military goals. Cognitive maneuver offers a promising option for the United States and its allies to exploit Russian vulnerabilities and undercut its new generation warfare model.

The purpose of this report is to apply a model developed by RAND Corporation researchers to explore adversaries' "will to fight," as a lens through which to analyze the threats posed by Russian private military

---

[2]   Candace Rondeaux, *Decoding the Wagner Group: Analyzing the Role of Private Military Security Contractors in Russian Proxy Warfare*, Washington, D.C.: New America, November 7, 2019, p. 20.

[3]   On the Russian concept of new generation warfare, see Linda Robinson, Todd C. Helmus, Raphael S. Cohen, Alireza Nader, Andrew Radin, Madeline Magnuson, and Katya Migacheva, *Modern Political Warfare: Current Practices and Possible Responses*, Santa Monica, Calif.: RAND Corporation, RR-1772-A, 2018, p. 42.

On private military companies (PMCs) and Russian hybrid warfare strategy, see Margarete Klein, *Private Military Companies: A Growing Instrument in Russia's Foreign and Security Policy Toolbox*, Helsinki, Finland: European Centre of Excellence for Countering Hybrid Threats, March 2019.

[4]   U.S. Department of Defense, *Summary of the 2018 National Defense Strategy of the United States of America: Sharpening the American Military's Competitive Edge*, January 19, 2018.

actors, focusing on the case study of the Syrian civil war between 2015 and 2019.[5] The ultimate aim is to help U.S. Army Special Operations Command (USASOC) and other U.S. military and government entities better assess (1) what motivates and demotivates private military contractors and the companies that hire them to fight; (2) what motivates and demotivates the Russian state government to utilize private military actors in Syria; and (3) what USASOC and other U.S. military and government entities can do to influence such activities.

In an attempt to elucidate U.S. opportunities to exploit the strengths and vulnerabilities associated with Russia's utilization of private military actors, this report explores key issues regarding private military actors' will to fight across multiple cases and time periods. In doing so, it focuses particularly but not exclusively on Russian private military actors, comparing and contrasting this relatively opaque, clientelistic case of military privatization with lessons learned from other cases of private military force use over the past several decades.

This topic is critically important for several reasons. First, the entire U.S. national security apparatus should be concerned about Russia's increasing deployment of private military actors worldwide, as such activity allows Russia to expand its military footprint while maintaining plausible deniability and, therefore, relative opacity both in major combat operations and in the competitive space short of armed conflict. Although Russia's use of private military actors is quickly becoming a global phenomenon, prior to the invasion of Ukraine in 2022, it

---

[5] For the purposes of this report, the phrase *private military actors* comprises both PMCs and individual private military contractor personnel. In this transnational industry, the two are related but also distinct. For example, Russian PMCs sometimes hire non-Russian nationals and sell their services to non-Russian firms and clients. Thus, it is critical to explore these actors' will to fight at both the corporate and individual levels. In the academic and policy literature, the term *PMC* is often conflated with both *private security company* (PSC) and *private military and security company* (PMSC). However, the distinction appears to be that PSCs provide security and combat-related services only, whereas *PMC* and *PMSC* are broader terms encompassing all the services marketed by these companies, including security and combat-related services. In this report, we refer simply to *PMCs* or *private military actors*, except when quoting from sources that use different terminology. Notably, Russia's primary private military actor, the Wagner Group, began as a more-traditional PMC, but it has essentially evolved into a state-affiliated paramilitary or auxiliary force in the years since this research was originally conducted.

had been most visible—and, arguably, had the greatest impact on conflict outcomes—in Syria. The U.S. Army needs to be well informed regarding Russian private military actors' characteristics, activities, motives, and vulnerabilities in the Syrian context to effectively coordinate future operations involving such actors.

All U.S. Army forces should be aware of Russian private military actors because of their potential participation in major combat operations or other direct operations in theaters of conflict. USASOC has a unique role in combating these forces, a result of both the positioning of USASOC-aligned forces globally and the particular skill sets of these forces. Army psychological operations, civil affairs, and special operations personnel are likely to be on the front lines, competing with or battling such opaque forces in the gray zone below the threshold of armed conflict. Therefore, it is essential for USASOC-aligned forces to comprehensively understand Russian private military actors and their roles, as well as possible methods for exploiting their vulnerabilities.

To that end, this report addresses the following research questions:

1. Who are the relevant actors in the Russian private military sphere for the purposes of understanding best how to influence these forces' will to fight?
2. What factors are most relevant to Russian private military actors' will to fight?
3. How do Russian private military actors compare with their current and historical Western counterparts, and what lessons can be drawn from these comparative cases to inform U.S. opportunities to defeat adversary-employed private military actors?

Cognitive Maneuver

As explained in USASOC's explorations of cognitive maneuver, the best way to win wars may be to use force in a multidomain context to achieve cognitive objectives—to change minds, to change behaviors, to win.[6] In general terms,

> maneuver is a principle of Joint operations that involves the employment of forces in the operational area through movement in combination with fires to achieve a position of advantage in respect to the enemy.[7]

In the land domain, military forces conduct combined arms maneuver, including envelopment, turning movement, frontal attack, penetration, infiltration, and flank attack.[8] Cognitive maneuver occurs in the human domain and aims to shape contextual conditions and influence decisionmaking. USASOC defines *cognitive maneuver* as

> the tactics of a campaign to shape the conditions of the global environment and influence actors' decision-making behaviors. We shape and influence to continually maintain positions of advantage, adapting to the changing nature and character of conflict.[9]

This is a natural outgrowth of efforts to operate in the human domain, in which "evolving operational demands require a force that is capable of impacting human decisionmaking and associated behavior and focus campaign design on creating desired effects to achieve success across all domains."[10]

Note that cognitive maneuver is related to cognitive aspects of military operations, which focus on the three mental functions that

---

[6] U.S. Army Special Operations Command, *Expanding Maneuver in the Early 21st Century Security Environment*, January 12, 2017.

[7] U.S. Army Special Operations Command, *Cognitive Maneuver for the Contemporary and Future Strategic Operating Environment*, May 31, 2016, p. 2.

[8] Robert A. Warburg, U.S. Army Special Operations Command, "Cognitive Maneuver for the Contemporary and Future Strategic Operating Environment," briefing, June 21, 2016.

[9] U.S. Army Special Operations Command, 2016.

[10] U.S. Special Operations Command, *Operating in the Human Domain*, version 1.0, August 3, 2015.

influence the formation of perception, intent, decisionmaking, and behavior: (1) *cognition*, which refers to modes of knowledge and information processing; (2) *affect*, which refers to emotion and feeling; and (3) *conation*, which refers to impulse, yearning, and striving to carry out an act.[11]

RAND's will-to-fight model draws on these explorations of how best to conceive of cognitive maneuver and seeks to elucidate the cognitive levers that may be relevant to various actors' will to fight in a range of circumstances.

Background on the Will-to-Fight Model

RAND's will-to-fight model, designed to analyze the military units of nation-states, includes 29 multifaceted cognitive factors that influence the will to fight of military units.

A primary goal of this assessment approach is to add purpose, structure, and credibility to what is often derided as a subjective process.[12] Ideally, further exploration and modification of the will-to-fight model and tool will lead to a holistic combat effectiveness assessment approach that integrates both the tangible and intangible factors of warfare.

Understanding the will to fight of any adversary requires assessing the factors that influence that adversary's forces. Factor-by-factor assessment is the most realistic, practical, and feasible way to assess the disposition of a military organization or unit to fight, act, or persevere. It is necessary to accept at the outset that finite clarity is out of reach. Furthermore, as stated earlier, there is no single factor or small

---

[11] Allison Astorino-Courtois, ed., *A Cognitive Capabilities Agenda: A Multi-Step Approach for Closing DoD's Cognitive Capability Gap*, Washington, D.C.: Joint Staff, Strategic Multi-Layer Assessment Office, October 2017; Patricia DeGennaro, "The Power of Cognitive Maneuver: Don't Underestimate Its Value," *Small Wars Journal*, September 19, 2017.

[12] See Ben Connable, *Embracing the Fog of War: Assessment and Metrics in Counterinsurgency*, Santa Monica, Calif.: RAND Corporation, MG-1086-DOD, 2012, and Ben Connable, Michael J. McNerney, William Marcellino, Aaron Frank, Henry Hargrove, Marek N. Posard, S. Rebecca Zimmerman, Natasha Lander, Jasen J. Castillo, and James Sladden, *Will to Fight: Analyzing, Modeling, and Simulating the Will to Fight of Military Units*, Santa Monica, Calif.: RAND Corporation, RR-2341-A, 2018.

set of key factors that can explain will to fight in any one case or in general. Instead, understanding will to fight is a process of factor-by-factor assessment with the goal of identifying strengths that might be reinforced and weaknesses that need to be shored up through security force assistance.

Figure 1.1 shows the will-to-fight model containing 29 major factors and 61 subfactors. All are derived from a nine-part, mixed-methods research effort, the results of which were published in the 2018 RAND report *Will to Fight: Analyzing, Modeling, and Simulating the Will to Fight of Military Units*.[13] The model helps focus the analysis of each factor at four different levels and along three broad dimensions: At the levels of the individual, unit, organization, state, and society, and along the dimensions of motivation, capability, and cultural factors. For example, unit competence is assessed as a capability, while societal identity is assessed as a cultural factor.[14] Most of the factors have associated subfactors, which are designed to help break down the analysis and categorize the evidence. For example, organizational control consists of methods of coercion, persuasion, and the cultural approach to discipline.[15] All factors are more or less *durable* in battle, rated high, mid, or low. Durability reflects the likelihood that factors might change over the course of a single battle or over a short series of battles. All the factors collectively help describe the unit's or organization's disposition to fight in a prospective battle.

---

[13] Connable et al., 2018.

[14] Unit competence is defined by unit skills, training, and performance. Skills indicate the ability of individuals and units to perform tasks. According to the will-to-fight model, "Training is the methods and capabilities used to build and maintain skills. Performance is the demonstration of skills. All components of competence can build or erode confidence and, therefore, disposition to fight" (Connable et al., 2018, p. 80).

In the will-to-fight model, identity "includes social and personal identity. It is the commitment to an identity (e.g., expectations about what a soldier does) or sense of self-search for satisfaction" (Connable et al., 2018, p. 54).

[15] Control "is the method of obtaining obedience to orders and pursuit of mission objectives. Control relies on a mix of coercion and persuasion, and it is reflected in discipline" (Connable et al., 2018, pp. 79–80).

Figure 1.1
The Military Will-to-Fight Model

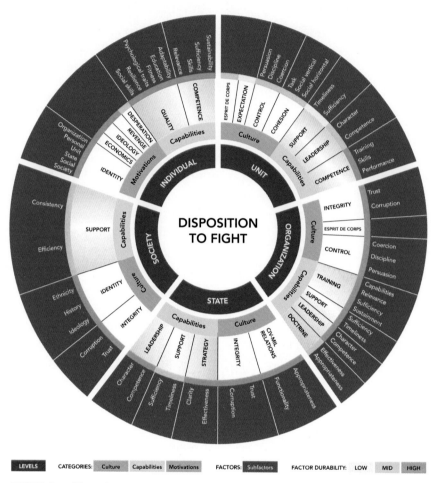

LEVELS   CATEGORIES: Culture Capabilities Motivations   FACTORS: Subfactors   FACTOR DURABILITY: LOW   MID   HIGH

SOURCE: Connable, et al., 2018, p. 111, Figure 2.34.

Each factor in the model represents a line of influence on the disposition to fight. Every factor is interdependent in some way. Organizational leadership affects unit leadership, which affects esprit de corps, unit support, cohesion, and so on.[16] In an ideal world, this model would be fully interactive and dynamic. There would be a theory-driven way to show every relational value between every factor, as well as a way to calculate all those dynamic relationships to generate a finding. As of mid-2023, no field of scientific endeavor had come close to cracking the code on this kind of interwoven human complexity. Therefore, the RAND model and this report pursue a clearer understanding of each factor, along with trends across factors.

Another way to view the model and factors is in table form. Table 1.1 shows the same factors, subfactors, levels, and categories aligned vertically and horizontally, with factors shaded.

---

[16] *Leadership* in the model is defined, described, and has the same subfactors at both the unit and organizational levels. "Leadership is the act of a single person in authority directing and encouraging the behavior of soldiers to accomplish a military mission." Leadership subfactors are competence and character, "and leaders connect with soldiers and other leaders through vertical cohesion." However, the description of organizational leadership notes, "Vertical cohesion between units and the organization's leadership is weaker and more distant than at the small-unit level," and "assessment and analysis of organizational influences on will to fight might require an examination of several levels of vertical leadership" (Connable et al., 2018, pp. 71, 88).

Relevant to all analyses of military will to fight in that loyalty to an organization influences individuals' and units' will to fight, "*Esprit de corps* is a French term generally translated as 'group spirit.' It is also called *élan* or *pride*, and it is often referred to simply as *esprit* (spirit). Members of a particular unit develop part of their individual identity in relation to the unit and to the organization." Acknowledging that it is a factor at every level of an organization, the will-to-fight model ties esprit to "the fighting spirit of a unit and an ardor or eagerness to pursue a cause or task," adding, "It captures a confidence in battle prowess and success, and concepts of elite membership." (Connable et al., 2018, pp. 77–78, 88).

Unit support "is the sufficiency and timeliness of equipment, supplies, weapons, medical assistance, fires, food, water, and other things the unit needs to accomplish its missions" (Connable et al., 2018, p. 82).

Cohesion includes both task cohesion and social cohesion at the unit level. Task cohesion is "a commitment to collective goals," whereas social cohesion "is bonding based on friendship, trust, or other aspects of interpersonal relationships," formed through, for example, "shared experience and hardship." In the model, "Social cohesion in the standard model of military group cohesion includes both horizontal (peer) and vertical (leader) bonds" (Connable et al., 2018, pp. 65–66).

Table 1.1
Will-to-Fight Model Factors and Subfactors

Level	Category	Factors	Subfactors
Individual	Individual motivations	Desperation	
		Revenge	
		Ideology	
		Economics	
	Individual capabilities	Individual identity	Personal, social, unit, state, organization, and society
		Quality	Fitness, resilience, education, adaptability, social skills, psychological traits
		Individual competence	Skills, relevance, sufficiency, and sustainability
Unit	Unit culture	Unit cohesion	Social vertical, social horizontal, and task
		Expectation	
		Unit control	Coercion, persuasion, and discipline
		Unit esprit de corps	
	Unit capabilities	Unit competence	Performance, skills, and training
		Unit support	Sufficiency and timeliness
		Unit leadership	Competence and character

Table 1.1—Continued

Level	Category	Factors	Subfactors
Organization	Organizational culture	Organizational control	Coercion, persuasion, and discipline
		Organizational esprit de corps	
		Organizational integrity	Corruption and trust
	Organizational capabilities	Organizational training	Capabilities, relevance, sufficiency, and sustainment
		Organizational support	Sufficiency and timeliness
		Doctrine	Appropriateness and effectiveness
		Organizational leadership	Competence and character
State	State culture	Civil-military relations	Appropriateness and functionality
		State integrity	Corruption and trust
	State capabilities	State support	Sufficiency and timeliness
		State strategy	Clarity and effectiveness
		State leadership	Competence and character
Society	Societal culture	Societal identity	Ideology, ethnicity, and history
		Societal integrity	Corruption and trust
	Societal capabilities	Societal support	Consistency and efficiency

SOURCE: Connable et al., 2018, pp. 41–42, Table 2.3.

NOTE: See Connable et al., 2018 for detailed definitions of each factor.

Even a quick review of the factors shows the holism inherent in the assessment approach. It includes a range of military-specific cultural factors, motivations, and capabilities, as well as a broad array of factors exogenous—but also critical—to understanding the will to fight of a military force. It includes analyses of such material factors as the quantity and quality of military equipment (under unit support, organizational support, and state support) and nonmaterial factors, such as training, fitness, individual skills, and leadership, that are often woven into existing combat effectiveness assessment tools.

Research Approach

To address the research questions that framed this study, we employed a multimethod qualitative approach. First, we drew on subject-matter expertise on PMC forces and the ways in which they differ from military units to identify an initial subset of factors in the will-to-fight model that were potentially applicable to this case. We narrowed down this subset of factors to those that appeared to capture the majority of the dynamics specific to PMC forces through a media analysis and scholarly literature review, conversations with subject-matter experts, and a limited number of semistructured interviews with foreign military personnel who had operational experience with Russian private military actors. In doing so, we identified a gap in the will-to-fight model that could reveal exploitable vulnerabilities relevant to cognitive maneuver: the health and well-being of private military contractors, something that appears to go unaddressed by either the Russian state or their corporate employers. We therefore propose the addition of an individual well-being factor.

Finally, we performed selective case study analyses of analogous instances of private military contractor employment to derive lessons learned and points at which particular individual, corporate, and client-state cognitive factors may be vulnerable to cognitive maneuver. It is critical to note that the following analysis is limited to identifying actors and cognitive factors that are relevant to Russia's use of private military forces—both in active conflicts and in other various areas of competition short of armed conflict—and pressure points that the United States could exploit.

The remainder of this report provides an overview of Russian private military actors and activity in Chapter Two. Chapter Three outlines the will-to-fight factors that are relevant to this case, details how the factors relate to Russian private military actors and activities, and describes theoretically exploitable vulnerabilities identified in our factor-based analysis. Chapter Four offers conclusions from our findings and recommendations for the U.S. government, U.S. Army, and USASOC specifically regarding future cognitive maneuver activities against Russian private military actors.

CHAPTER TWO

Russia's Private Military Actors

The rapid growth in Russia's employment of private military actors in recent years is notable and appears to be tied to the Russian state's overall efforts to quietly increase its global footprint below the threshold of armed conflict through hybrid warfare and strategic competition. In addressing the first research aims of this study, this chapter explores the question of *who* the relevant actors are in the Russian private military sphere for the purposes of understanding how best to influence their will to fight.

It is important to note Russia's roles as both a contracting state and a home state for contracted forces (i.e., it employs private military actors both domestically and abroad, and it exports private military services to other client states).[1] The distinction between Russia's import and export markets for private forces has become increasingly opaque, with the Russian state technically maintaining that the existence of private military companies and the use of their services are illegal in Russia, despite extensive evidence of close Russian state support and client relationships with particular firms.[2] Interestingly, prominent figures, including Russian president Vladimir Putin, have argued

---

[1] This exporting of private military support occurs through contracts with PMCs, such as the Wagner Group, and deployments of individual private military contractors.

[2] Michael Weiss, "The Case of the Keystone Cossacks," *Foreign Policy*, November 21, 2013; Kimberly Marten, "Russia's Use of Semi-State Security Forces: The Case of the Wagner Group," *Post-Soviet Affairs*, Vol. 35, No. 3, 2019.

for legalization, and a bill to legalize PMCs was proposed in Russia's Duma in 2018. It did not pass.[3]

Prior to 2014, foreign military experts and scholars of military privatization generally believed that the market for forces *exported* from Russia and Ukraine—that is, for individual contractors' and small firms' services purchased by non-Russian entities—was generally thought to be small in comparison to the markets in the United States and the United Kingdom. The market tended to operate through informal networks rather than large corporate structures, with sellers who were generally (but not exclusively) individuals or small companies. As they do today, buyers included a range of foreign states, international government organizations, and private individuals. In the early 2000s, the Russian press estimated that between 5,000 and 10,000 Russian and Ukrainian contractor personnel were providing transport support—and sometimes filled combat roles—for various foreign firms and other entities around the globe. Contractor personnel on the Russian export market at this time were involved primarily in piloting Russian and Soviet planes and, increasingly, acting as armed guards or paramilitary forces in conflict zones. At that time, aircraft pilots and experts were by far the most commonly contracted personnel from Russia and Ukraine.[4]

This export market should not be confused with the internal post-Soviet market for forces purchased by Russian entities to support operations abroad, but this appears to have been critical in driving the shape and character of present-day Russian private military actors. This market can trace its lineage back to counter-terror and counter-espionage units formed under the auspices of KGB development courses for officers following the dissolution of the Soviet Union—namely, Alpha Group and its sister unit Vympel (also known as Vega Group).

---

[3]   Sergey Sukhankin, *"Continuing War by Other Means": The Case of Wagner, Russia's Premier Private Military Company in the Middle East*, Washington, D.C.: Jamestown Foundation, July 13, 2018b.

[4]   Olivia Allison, "Informal but Diverse: The Market for Exported Force from Russia and Ukraine," in Molly Dunigan and Ulrich Petersohn, eds., *The Markets for Force: Privatization of Security Across World Regions*, Philadelphia, Pa.: University of Pennsylvania Press, 2015, pp. 88–89.

Alpha Group and Vympel, in turn, have ties to World War II partisan warfare units and the creation of specialized irregular reconnaissance task forces in the 1950s.[5]

The supply of skilled veterans and related corporate networks following the dissolution of the Soviet Union therefore drove the market to some extent. Yet, the foundations of the demand signal in the current Russian market are shaped by clientelism, in the form of private firms that emerged in the post–Cold War era to support the security needs of state energy companies, such as Gazprom, Tatneft, Stroytransgaz, Zarubezhneft, Rosneft, and Surgutneftgaz, all of which are, in turn, led by close associates of Russian president Vladimir Putin.[6] As Candace Rondeaux notes,

> The transition of elite security cadres from government service to private security overlapped with several phases of privatization and reorganization of state enterprises of strategic importance for Russia's export base. State-backed energy firms soon emerged as a key incubator for the PMSC industry. A few years after the Soviet collapse, [Russian president Boris] Yeltsin issued an executive decree that allowed Gazprom and Transneft to set up their own militarized armies to protect newly built infrastructure. Transneft and Gazprom subsequently joined a wave of state-run firms in the finance and energy sectors that staffed their specialized security divisions with former top KGB officers at the time.[7]

Corporate demand for privatized security services continued to grow: By 2007, Gazprom employed 20,000 or more contracted personnel to secure its operations. Simultaneously, Putin initiated a broader, quiet privatization push between 2005 and 2007, giving control of major Russian exporting industries to politicians with state security ties and to longtime associates with roots in the KGB or its modern successor, the Russian Federal Security Service (FSB).[8]

---

[5] Rondeaux, 2019, pp. 25–26.

[6] Rondeaux, 2019, pp. 20–29.

[7] Rondeaux, 2019, pp. 28–29.

[8] Rondeaux, 2019, p. 27.

It was against this backdrop of Russian force privatization that Dmitry Utkin, former commander of Glavnoye Razvedyvatelnoye Upravleniye (GRU) Spetsnaz—Russian special forces units attached to the chief intelligence directorate of the Russian general staff—is reported to have founded the Wagner Group in 2014. Utkin was reportedly fascinated with Nazi Germany and chose the name "Wagner" in homage to one of Hitler's favorite composers.[9] Wagner contractors took part in the 2014 annexation of Crimea and have fought in Donbass, in eastern Ukraine. In fall 2015, when Moscow launched its military intervention in Syria, Wagner deployed more than 2,000 personnel there.[10]

Though increasingly notorious, the Wagner Group is just one of several known Russian PMCs that operate abroad or have done so in the relatively recent past. In addition to the Wagner Group, the following Russian private military actors have been cited in traditional media and online reporting since 2001:

- Anti-Terror Orel
- Slavonic Corps
- Moran Security Group
- RSB Group
- E.N.O.T. Corps
- MAR
- DOBRANDR
- Turan
- Centre R
- ATK Group
- Tigr Top-Rent Security
- Cossacks
- Patriot.[11]

---

[9] Mike Giglio, "Inside the Shadow War Fought by Russian Mercenaries," BuzzFeed News, April 17, 2019.

[10] Metin Gurcan, "Private Military Companies: Moscow's Other Army in Syria," Al-Monitor, November 30, 2017.

[11] Marten (2019) has highlighted that the RSB Group posts conflicting claims on its website that it "does not participate in armed conflicts" but can produce 1,000 former Russian

Media and scholarly reports detail, with a mix of hard evidence and speculation, that contractors working under the auspices of one or more of these companies have operated in Iraq, Afghanistan, Ukraine, Syria, Libya, Chechnya, Tajikistan, Yemen, and Burundi, in some cases as far back as the 1990s. This is in addition to reported Wagner Group operations in Ukraine, Syria, Sudan, the Central African Republic, Madagascar, Libya, Mozambique, Mali, and Venezuela.[12]

Indeed, by summer 2017, the Wagner Group *alone* may have employed as many as 5,000 contractors just to Syria. That number allegedly jumped dramatically from approximately 1,000 a year earlier.[13] Other reports as of early 2018 provided more-precise numbers, with a slightly lower count of 4,840 Wagner contractors, though it is unclear whether all were deployed to Syria at that time.[14] And as of early 2023, approximately 50,000 Wagner contractors were reportedly operating in Ukraine.

Industry Structure in Context

Russian private military actors and their relationships to the Russian state and Russian society differ in some ways from historical cases of

---

military officers ready to take up arms in under a week. The group is rumored to have operated in Libya and claims to provide security functions for Russian companies around the globe in coordination with the FSB. For more information on E.N.O.T. Corps, see Sukhankin, 2018b. Scholars and journalists have speculated that the Turan's existence may have been completely fabricated. Marten (2019) reports that a Russian watchdog organization, the Conflict Intelligence Team, demonstrated through comparative photographic evidence that Turan, supposedly operating in Syria, was fake. Nonetheless, several Russian media outlets repeated claims about Turan's involvement in Syria as if they were true. Marten (2019) mentions Patriot in passing; definitive evidence of this firm's existence remains elusive.

[12] Browne, 2019; Lister, Shukla, and Ward, 2019; Flanagan, 2019; Marten, 2019.

[13] Sarah Fainberg, *Russian Spetsnaz: Contractors and Volunteers in the Syrian Conflict*, Paris: French Institute of International Relations, Russie.Nei.Visions No. 105, December 2017; Neil Hauer, "Putin Has a New Secret Weapon in Syria: Chechens," *Foreign Policy*, May 4, 2017.

[14] Sergey Sukhankin, "War, Business and 'Hybrid' Warfare: The Case of the Wagner Private Military Company (Part Two)," *Eurasia Daily Monitor*, Vol. 15, No. 61, April 23, 2018a.

military privatization, and scholars and journalists studying these cases have focused on such distinctions and their implications as a departure from historical precedent.[15] However, in other ways, Russia's use of private military actors bears striking similarities to historical cases (in terms of both the purchase and sale of such services) involving the United States, United Kingdom, and South Africa, among other countries. Indeed, Russian private military actors constitute a hybrid between PMSCs and contractors emanating from the heretofore dominant states in the modern-day privatized security and military services market (such as the United States, United Kingdom, Australia, New Zealand, and South Africa) and the historical "mercenaries" with whom they are often grouped in terms of terminology.

A widely agreed-upon definition of the term *mercenary* is elusive, with scholars and analysts arguing over many of the most basic components of mercenarism.[16] Most traditional conceptions of mercenaries involve a profit motivation or a foreign component and may depend on the degree to which they engage in public versus

---

[15] See, for instance, Anna Borshchevskaya, *Russian Private Military Companies: Continuity and Evolution of the Model*, Philadelphia, Pa.: Foreign Policy Research Institute, December 2019; Nathaniel Reynolds, *Putin's Not-So-Secret Mercenaries: Patronage, Geopolitics, and the Wagner Group*, Washington, D.C.: Carnegie Endowment for International Peace, July 8, 2019.

[16] Molly Dunigan, *Victory for Hire: Private Security Companies' Impact on Military Effectiveness*, Palo Alto, Calif.: Stanford University Press, 2011, p. 15. Article 47.2 of Additional Protocol I of the Geneva Conventions defines a *mercenary* as

> any person who
>
> (a) is specially recruited locally and abroad in order to fight in an armed conflict;
>
> (b) does, in fact, take a direct part in hostilities;
>
> (c) is motivated to take part in the hostilities essentially by the desire for private gain and, in fact, is promised by or on behalf of a Party to the conflict material compensation substantially in excess of that promised or paid to combatants of similar rank and functions in the armed forces of that Party;
>
> (d) is neither a national of a Party to the conflict nor a resident of territory controlled by a Party to the conflict;
>
> (e) is not a member of the armed forces of a Party to the conflict; and
>
> (f) has not been sent by a State which is not a Party to the conflict on official duty as a member of its armed forces.

private violence, on a historical spectrum. Not quite mercenaries, auxiliary forces (troops hired out in units by their rulers to serve in foreign conflicts) are considered to be more mercenary-like than modern-day private military companies based in Western countries, both because they tend to be less attached to the cause for which they are fighting and because they are less often subject to legitimate control by the state actors in question. Historical examples of auxiliary forces include the Hessian forces hired to fight for the British in the American Revolution and the *condottieri* hired by Italian city-states in the 13th–15th centuries.[17]

Western PMCs, in contrast, are less mercenary-like than are most historical examples of mercenaries and auxiliary forces and have several notable characteristics distinguishing them from traditional, historically grounded concepts of mercenaries. Such characteristics include the following:

- Western PMC personnel are, by definition, backed by a corporate infrastructure designed to select, train, and deploy them. This corporate infrastructure similarly bids on contracts and, in most cases, has a professional portfolio detailing its performance on previous contracts.

---

[17] Dunigan, 2011; Joseph Jay Deiss, *Captains of Fortune: Profiles of Six Italian Condottieri*, New York: Thomas Y. Crowell Company, 1967; Daniel Waley, *The Italian City-Republics*, London: World University Library, 1969; C. C. Bayley, *War and Society in Renaissance Florence: The "De Militia" of Leonardo Bruni*, Toronto: University of Toronto Press, 1961; Eugene B. Smith, "The New Condottieri and US Policy: The Privatization of Conflict and its Implications," *Parameters*, Vol. 32, No. 4, Winter 2002–2003; Michael Mallett, *Mercenaries and Their Masters: Warfare in Renaissance Italy*, London: Bodley Head, 1974; William Caferro, "Italy and the Companies of Adventure in the Fourteenth Century," *The Historian*, Vol. 58, No. 4, June 1996; Edward J. Lowell, *The Hessians and the Other German Auxiliaries of Great Britain in the Revolutionary War*, New York: Harper and Brothers, 1884, chapt. 2; Joseph George Rosengarten, *A Defence of the Hessians*, reprint, Philadelphia, Pa.: Historical Society of Pennsylvania, July 1899; Johann Ernst Prechtel, *A Hessian Officer's Diary of the American Revolution*, Bruce E. Burgoyne, trans., Bowie, Md.: Heritage Books, 1994; Rodney Atwood, *The Hessians: Mercenaries from Hessen-Kassel in the American Revolution*, New York: Cambridge University Press, 1980; Mark Mayo Boatner III, *Encyclopedia of the American Revolution*, New York: David McKay Publications, 1969; Johann Georg Zinn, journal entry in Bruce E. Burgoyne, ed. and trans., *Enemy Views: The American Revolutionary War as Recorded by the Hessian Participants*, Westminster, Md.: Heritage Books, 1996.

- The modern private military industry in Western states is unique in its scale and transnational nature. Indeed, many PMCs have the capability to hire hundreds of personnel representing a range of nationalities on short notice.
- Virtually all reputable U.S.- and UK-based firms openly compete for government contracts and espouse a company ideology in line with the ideals of the United States and its Western allies.[18]
- Some but not all Western PMCs do indeed make both explicit and implicit attempts to shape foreign policy. In this sense, the degree of state control over modern Western PMCs seems to be rather reciprocal. The former Blackwater Worldwide is a prime example of this phenomenon.[19]
- Western companies in the industry adhere to several pieces of regulatory guidance aimed at increasing contractors' compliance with international humanitarian law and instituting quality management systems for business operations at the corporate level. Relevant guidance includes the Montreux Document, the International Code of Conduct for Private Security Service Providers, and the American National Standards Institute's PSC.1 Standard.[20]

---

[18] Western PMC firms have nonetheless been the subject of numerous and at times high-profile reports of a lack of accountability and excessive use of force, suggesting that espousal of U.S. and allied ideals is not necessarily equivalent to adherence to related principles of international humanitarian law and the laws of war. See, for instance, Sarah K. Cotton, Ulrich Petersohn, Molly Dunigan, Q Burkhart, Megan Zander-Cotugno, Edward O'Connell, and Michael Webber, *Hired Guns: Views About Armed Contractors in Operation Iraqi Freedom*, Santa Monica, Calif: RAND Corporation, MG-987-SRF, 2010; Matt Apuzzo, "Blackwater Guards Found Guilty in 2007 Iraq Killings," *New York Times*, October 22, 2014.

[19] Acting almost like a nongovernmental organization or think tank, Blackwater's Global Peacekeeping and Stability Operations Institute made the case for a public-private partnership between the U.S. military and PMCs in conducting peacekeeping operations. See Dunigan, 2011, chapt. 1.

[20] The International Code of Conduct contains "standards and principles for the responsible provision of private security services" that are tied to international law and rules for companies that are members of the International Code of Conduct Association. (See International Code of Conduct Association, "About Us," webpage, undated.) The code is an outgrowth of the 2008 Montreux Document, a collaboration between the International Committee of the Red Cross and the Swiss Federal Department of Foreign Affairs that brought together repre-

Despite these characteristics, Western PMCs do arguably resemble mercenaries to a much greater extent than do regular, state-sanctioned forces.[21] Russian private military actors, on the other hand, are somewhat closer to auxiliaries than Western PMCs. In her detailed case study of the Wagner Group, Kimberly Marten refers to Russian private military companies as

> "semi-state" informal security organizations that have an opaque relationship with the Russian state, characterized by partial recognition and hazy contracting, sometimes in the face of apparent illegality. The vast majority of their members are recently retired veterans from one or another Russian state security force, but some groups have also attracted pro-Russian fighters from other post-Soviet states and Serbia as members.[22]

Figure 2.1 presents a notional comparison between Russian and Western private military actors relative to state, mercenary, and auxiliary forces.

---

sentatives of 17 governments and "drew widely on the knowledge of industry representatives, academic experts, and nongovernmental organizations."

The Montreux Document describes itself as "an intergovernmental statement [that] clearly articulating the most pertinent international legal obligations [of states] with regard to PMSCs," as well as the legal status of these personnel. See International Committee of the Red Cross and Federal Department of Foreign Affairs of Switzerland, *The Montreux Document on Pertinent International Legal Obligations and Good Practices for States Related to Operations of Private Military and Security Companies During Armed Conflict*, Geneva, Switzerland, September 17, 2008.

The PSC.1 Standard, published by the American National Standards Institute and ASIS International, provides detailed, auditable requirements and guidance for PMCs, building on the Montreux Document and International Code of Conduct. See American National Standards Institute and ASIS International, *Management System for Quality of Private Security Company Operations: Requirements with Guidance*, Alexandria, Va.: ASIS International, American National Standard PSC.1-2012, 2012.

[21] Dunigan, 2011, p. 19; Anthony Mockler, The Mercenaries, New York: Macmillan, 1969; Janice E. Thomson, *Mercenaries, Pirates, and Sovereigns*, Princeton, N.J.: Princeton University Press, 1994; P. W. Singer, *Corporate Warriors: The Rise of the Privatized Military Industry*, Ithaca, N.Y.: Cornell University Press, 2003; Sarah Percy, *Mercenaries: The History of a Norm in International Relations*, Oxford, UK: Oxford University Press, 2007; Niccolò Machiavelli, The Prince, George Bull, trans., New York: Random House, 2003, chapt. XIII.

[22] Marten, 2019.

Figure 2.1
Notional Visualization of Russian and Western Private Military Actors on the Public-Private Spectrum of Participation in Military Operations

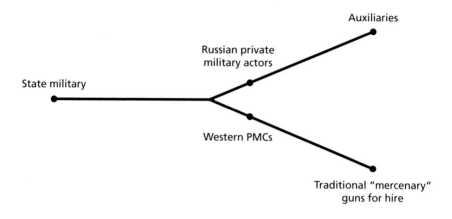

Interestingly, the Russian state also appears to take a somewhat contradictory stance on whether it considers private military actors to be state-sanctioned forces and has refused to grant legal recognition to PMCs. As president, Putin has decorated private military actors for their service, and wounded Wagner fighters were evacuated from Syrian battlefields to Russian military hospitals on Russian military planes.[23] Yet, Russian state military forces will not tend to wounded private military actors on the battlefield prior to evacuation, and the FSB has met Russian contractors at the airport when they arrive back in Russia—after they have ostensibly supported state-sponsored missions—to interrogate and arrest them.[24] This odd relationship between the Russian state and Russian private military actors speaks to these forces' greater similarity to auxiliaries as opposed to true mercenaries.

Marten notes that Russian private military actors have often functioned as force providers engaging in paramilitary or combat roles. This is another key distinction. Western PMCs provide a variety of services, including personal security details, training and advising, base support, logistical support, construction, weapon maintenance, transportation,

---

[23] Marten, 2019.

[24] Weiss, 2013; Marten, 2019.

communication, intelligence analysis, and risk analysis, in addition to a very small subset of actors engaged in paramilitary activities.[25]

Clearly, Western private military actors are not a perfect analogue for Russian private military actors. Table 2.1 summarizes the distinctions discussed in this chapter and prefaces several additional differences between the two types of forces that are elaborated in Chapter Three.

Scholars and analysts have been studying the dynamics of historical and modern Western private military actors for the past two decades, and the variables driving Western private military actors' will to fight and the concomitant markets for force are fairly well understood. Russian private military actors, on the other hand, are a relative black box. It therefore makes sense to perform a comparative analysis of Russian and Western private military actors to highlight possible points of influence related to Russia's use of these personnel. In line with our third research question, Chapter Three presents trends and dynamics associated with a number of historical instances of Western private military utilization in examining the factors motivating private military actors to fight.

These comparisons offer insights about potential pressure points for exploiting states' willingness to utilize private military forces, as well as the willingness of those forces and the companies that employ them to become embroiled in conflict themselves.

---

[25] Moshe Schwartz and Joyprada Swain, *Department of Defense Contractors in Afghanistan and Iraq: Background and Analysis*, Washington, D.C.: Congressional Research Service, R40764, May 2011, p. 16; Molly Dunigan, Carrie M. Farmer, Rachel M. Burns, Alison Hawks, and Claude Messan Setodji, *Out of the Shadows: The Health and Well-Being of Private Contractors Working in Conflict Environments*, Santa Monica, Calif.: RAND Corporation, RR-420-RC, 2013.

Table 2.1
Comparing Western and Russian Private Military Actors

Factor	Western Private Military Actors	Russian Private Military Actors
Individual-level motivations	Mix of economic and ideological (patriotic) incentives	Primarily economic incentives
Contractor personnel roles	Hired primarily to provide security/defense or combat support services (e.g., transport)	Often engage in direct combat in paramilitary roles; some engage in static site guarding
Pay and living/ working conditions	Treatment varies by nationality: TCNs and local nationals paid less and have less hospitable living/ working conditions	Treatment appears to vary by rank and military/government affiliation (e.g., personnel with FSB or GRU connections receive preferential treatment)
Recruitment	Transnational	Personnel drawn primarily from Russia, Serbia, Ukraine, and Moldova
PMC ideology	Aligned with Western values and goals; implicit and explicit attempts to shape policy	Indirect and opaque alignment with Russian state values and goals
Coordination with military forces	Evidence of coordination problems and tensions with military forces	Command-and-control (C2) template drawn from Russian armed forces might promote coordination (at least in the case of the Wagner Group)
Legal status and state recognition	Legal recognition and extensive corporate relationships with the U.S. Department of Defense (DoD)	No legal recognition

CHAPTER THREE

Applying the Will-to-Fight Model to Private Military Actors

Notably, the military will-to-fight model is not a perfect analogue for assessing the factors that motivate either individual private military contractors or PMCs or for assessing the factors that motivate the states that hire them. The model is premised on the organization of military units and relationships to their state and society; private military actors differ from military units both in their organization and in state government and societal perceptions of their role. Nonetheless, the military model is a useful baseline for understanding this population's will to fight. Five factors from the model are relevant to the private military sphere, but we suggest adding an additional factor that is particularly salient to this analysis: individual well-being.

This chapter discusses all six of these factors in relation to both Russia's use of private military actors and historical cases of predominantly Western military privatization. What follows is a deep dive into the motivations of a new ground force adversary that the United States is confronting in multiple theaters and in notably large numbers in Syria. As the Army considers Russian private military actors' motivations and how they align with these will-to-fight factors in the Syrian theater and elsewhere, it might identify new opportunities to greatly strengthen U.S. tactical, operational, and strategic positions against such forces.

Translating the Military Will-to-Fight Model to Private Military Actors

Translating the military will-to-fight model to the private military sphere required identifying several key distinctions between military units and private military actors. Again, the model explores the cognitive motivations of five levels of actors: individuals, units, organizations, the state, and society. However, the private military industry is a transnational phenomenon, crossing state borders and balancing the interests of business, government, military, and society in various ways. As noted in Chapter One, we employed a multimethod qualitative approach that drew on subject-matter expertise, media analysis, a scholarly literature review, conversations with subject-matter experts, and a limited number of semistructured interviews with foreign military personnel to (1) identify an initial subset of factors in the will-to-fight model that were applicable and (2) to narrow down this subset of applicable factors to those that appeared to capture the majority of the dynamics specific to Russian private military actors.

Through this research, we developed a private military will-to-fight model comprising factors at the **individual level** (contractor personnel themselves), the contractor operator **team level** (taking the place of the military unit), the **company level** (that is, the corporate entity employing the personnel and winning the contracts), the **state level**, and the **societal level**. There are three distinct types of "state" actors that are relevant to private military utilization: (1) the *client state* with which a PMC has a contract (i.e., the *contracting state*); (2) the *territorial state* on whose territory contractors operate; and (3) the *home states* from whose citizenry the contracting personnel are drawn.[1]

Figure 3.1 shows the five factors that we identified as particularly important for understanding the will to fight of private military actors—specifically, Russian private military actors. The figure also

---

[1] According to the 2008 Montreux Document, a *contracting state* is one that directly enters into a contract with a PMSC or one of its subcontractors. A *territorial state* is where a given PMSC operates, and a *home state* is where a given PMSC is registered or incorporated or its "principal place of management." (International Committee of the Red Cross and Federal Department of Foreign Affairs of Switzerland, 2008, p. 10).

Figure 3.1
Factors Relevant to Private Military Actors' Will to Fight

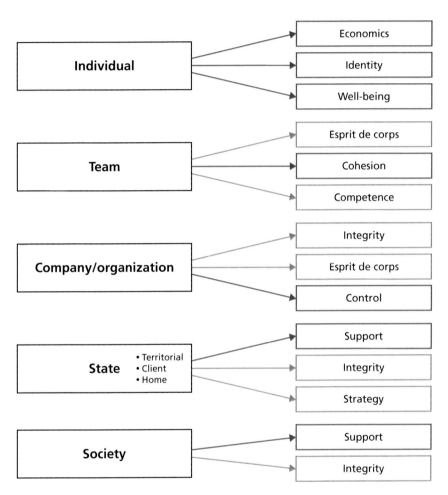

SOURCE: Identified factors draw on the military will-to-fight model described in Connable et al., 2018, with the exception of individual well-being, an addition suggested by this research.

NOTES: A red outline indicates a key factor that determines a Russian private military actor's will to fight: economic pressures, identity, individual well-being, unit cohesion, organizational control, and degree of support at the state and societal levels. The remaining factors (outlined in gray) are potentially relevant to the effectiveness of private military actors but were not decisive in motivating them to fight.

shows our modification to the will-to-fight model in the form of the additional individual-level factor of individual well-being. Key factors that determine Russian private military actors' will to fight are outlined in red. Although the remaining factors could be relevant, our research indicated that they were not decisive factors in motivating private military actors to fight. Detailed definitions of all the factors can be found in the appendix.

Individual-Level Factors
Identity
Identity in the military will-to-fight model includes both social and personal identity and is defined as "a commitment to an identity (e.g., expectations about what a soldier does) or sense of self-search for satisfaction."[2] In assessing private military actors' will to fight, identity and other individual-level factors may provide the best opportunity for U.S. military exploitation. In other words, the individual identities of contractor personnel vary, and they may not align with the expectations of the Russian state or the goals of a PMC's leadership in general or in relation to a particular contractor deployment. In the military will-to-fight model, "identity is both culturally obtained and unique within the individual: Each soldier forms a unique perspective on various influencing identities, and in doing so creates a separate unique identity that influences will to fight."[3] The impact of identity on will to fight is variable. However, detailed analyses of private military contractors' individual identities can provide insight into potential vulnerabilities in their will to fight.

   Identity is a complex concept in the private military sphere, often characterized on the Western side of the industry—which actively recruits personnel with military experience—by a desire to apply military-acquired skills in a civilian career field, and to do so lucratively.[4] Patriotism has also been found to be a key component of identity in the

---

[2] Connable et al., 2018, p. 54.

[3] Connable et al., 2018, p. 53.

[4] *Western* actors, as defined here, are based in or operate primarily from the United States, United Kingdom, Canada, South Africa, Australia, New Zealand, or NATO countries; they

Western private military industry, where most firms strive to actively align themselves with the rhetoric, goals, and ideology espoused by Western state clients.[5]

Alison Hawks points out that a key distinction between military identity and what *identity* means for actors in the private military industry, as well as what makes the latter so difficult to define: "Security contracting is the culmination of experience. It is not a new skill industry in which distinctive skills and qualities are developed for purposes of identification."[6] Complicating any definition of *identity* for private military actors is the variation in contract terms and lengths; contractors move between teams, clients, employers, and countries. By its nature, the industry transcends national boundaries in the personnel it employs, the corporate players that dominate at any given time, and the public and private clients it serves.

Drawing on data from a survey and interviews with former U.S. and UK service members who were employed as private security contractor personnel, Hawks found that these personnel sought employment in the private military industry out of a desire for an environment in which they would be (1) understood using a common language, (2) recognized for specific skills and competencies, and (3) able to engage in work that gave them purpose. For those who had been out of the military for less than six months before becoming a security contractor, Hawks identified the strongest motives for seeking such work as a desire for environmental continuity, autonomy in contrast to a perceived lack of autonomy during military service, and social mobility through economic gain—such as paying for education, homeownership, and debt eradication. For Western contractors in the study sample who had spent more than six months in civilian life before becoming a security contractor, the strongest motives for joining the industry were a desire to return to a remembered experience, or "get

---

also include local and third-country actors hired by the governments of the United States, United Kingdom, Canada, Australia, New Zealand, or closely allied countries.

[5]   Dunigan, 2011.

[6]   Alison Hawks, "I've Got Soul, but I'm Not a Soldier," *St. Antony's International Review*, Vol. 9, No. 2, February 2014, pp. 72–73.

back in the game"; to have others recognize the skills and competence acquired during their military career; to feel a sense of belonging; and to receive relatively substantial economic remuneration for their skills.[7]

The Russian private military actors operating in Syria and elsewhere are so shadowy and elusive that it is difficult to definitively confirm the various components of their identity. Yet, we can piece together a partial picture from multiple reports by Yevgeny Shabaev, a former Russian military officer who has become an advocate for members of the Wagner Group and other Russian PMCs and claims to be in regular contact with these personnel. In a 2019 media interview, Shabaev claimed that Russian contractors are driven solely by monetary incentives rather than patriotic identity: "The system is based on personal financial interests, not on military sense. There is not any patriotism. There is only financial interest."[8] Shabaev also noted that state coercion may play a role, with some fighters recruited directly out of prison and with few other options open to them.[9]

In these ways, personnel employed by Russian PMCs may be somewhat distinct from their Western counterparts. Then again, they may not be; Russian fighters quoted in the press have espoused patriotism to Russia:

> There is a bigger motivation. If you are fighting under a Russian flag, with a Russian weapon, even if you are eating moldy food and are 10,000 kilometers from home, you are nonetheless fighting for Russia.[10]

We know that most contractors who worked for Russian firms through early 2020 were of Russian, Serbian, Ukrainian, or Moldovan descent; Western firms, in contrast, tend to draw on a transnational

---

[7] Hawks, 2014, pp. 76–77.

[8] Giglio, 2019.

[9] Borshchevskaya, 2019.

[10] Sergei Khazov-Cassia and Robert Coalson, "Russian Mercenaries: Vagner Commanders Describe Life Inside the 'Meat Grinder,'" Radio Free Europe/Radio Liberty, March 14, 2018.

hiring pool.[11] Yet, up until the massive deployment of Wagner fight-ers in Ukraine in 2022 and 2023, most Russian private military actors were similar to their Western counterparts in that they tended to be either military veterans or former officers of the military intelligence agency (GRU) or federal security agency (FSB), and most are recruited through informal and online veteran networks.[12]

Existing knowledge of the Wagner Group provides some idea of how Russian PMCs were organized at the time of their involvement in Syria; there is some evidence that such an organizational structure has continued in the Wagner deployments to Ukraine in 2022 and 2023. There appear to be multiple levels of Wagner forces: essentially, the "cannon-fodder" (untrained, unskilled, force multipliers), semiama-teurs (recruited through veteran and Cossack networks), and a highly skilled officer level. Indeed, Wagner fighters have speculated in media interviews that the Russian state uses particularly dangerous operations as a "meat grinder," sending the most ideologically minded recruits in an effort to purge potentially disruptive elements from its own borders:

> There is a rumor that [Wagner] is a so-called "meat-grinder" proj-ect. What is to be done with those who fought in Donbas? With the idiots from the first wave who are real ideologues? These are scary people who could catalyze society. They can cause trouble like yeast in bread. But in Syria, you can help the interests of the country and get rid of some yeast at the same time. That's what some people are saying. And probably there is something to it.[13]

---

[11] Ori Swed and Thomas Crosbie, "Who Are the Private Contractors in Iraq and Afghani-stan?" *Military Times*, March 14, 2019.

[12] Andrew Linder, "Russian Private Military Companies in Syria and Beyond," *New Perspec-tives in Foreign Policy*, No. 16, Fall 2018; Reynolds, 2019. This, of course, shifted in 2022 and 2023, with the massive use of Wagner fighters in Ukraine; an estimated 40,000 person-nel were reportedly recruited directly from Russian prisons ("Russia's Wagner Mercenaries Halt Prisoner Recruitment Campaign—Prigozhin," Reuters, February 9, 2023).

[13] Khazov-Cassia and Coalson, 2018.

Other Wagner fighters have impressive military records.[14] There are indications that the more highly skilled forces are being recruited directly out of the FSB, where personnel are thought to be more capable than those in the GRU.[15]

On the whole, then, it appears that contractors operating on Russian PMC contracts are typically Eastern European, perhaps patriotic, and most likely have a background in military or intelligence skill sets that they are seeking to apply to lucrative work beyond the military. This assessment implies that, in general, some portion of these contractor personnel falls into a limited demographic with narrowly defined and largely transactional incentives that drive their will to fight. Therefore, if offered other or more promising employment opportunities utilizing these skill sets, they might be vulnerable to enticement away from the ranks of these firms.

Individual Well-Being

Individual well-being is not included in the military will-to-fight model. However, a high prevalence of deployment-related physical and mental health conditions in transnational contractor populations, coupled with a lack of long-term mental and physical health care among these populations, make this factor a major point of distinction between private military actors and state-run military forces. Defined as "the state of being happy, healthy, or prosperous," individual well-being is relevant to both physical and mental health.[16] A minimal level of economic security is necessary to ensure physical and mental health and, hence, well-being. Challenges to individual well-being may decrease will to fight, as well as effective occupational functioning in theater.[17]

Indeed, because state-sanctioned military forces often have long-term health insurance coverage and other benefits associated with government employment, they are better able to address deployment-

---

[14] Reynolds, 2019.

[15] Sukhankin, 2018a.

[16] Merriam-Webster, "Well-Being," *Merriam-Webster.com Dictionary*, undated.

[17] See, for example, Dunigan et al., 2013, on the relationship between various aspects of deployment-related mental health and occupational functioning.

related health concerns than contractors, for whom insurance and benefits—when offered at all—do not typically extend beyond the short duration of a contract.[18] Moreover, media and scholarly reporting indicate that Russian private military actors in Syria and beyond have suffered from health-related effects of deployment, pointing to the possibility that this factor represents exploitable vulnerabilities. We therefore determined that an individual well-being factor would be a useful addition to explore and analyze private military contractors' will to fight at the individual level. Because these personnel are often transient actors in the industry, interested in short-term but lucrative employment, and frequently move between contracts and companies, the cognitive factors motivating them to fight at the individual level have a particularly strong potential for exploitation.

Prior research indicates that contractors worldwide suffer quietly from deployment-related mental health problems, such as posttraumatic stress disorder (PTSD) and depression, in greater numbers than either U.S. or UK military veterans. A 2013 survey of a transnational sample of 660 contractors found that 25 percent met criteria for probable PTSD, 18 percent screened positive for depression, and 10 percent reported high-risk drinking.[19] By comparison, the proportions among U.S. military troops deployed to Iraq or Afghanistan at that time were estimated at 4–20 percent for PTSD, 5–37 percent for depression, and 5–39 percent for alcohol abuse.[20] Rates of PTSD were lower among UK military personnel, with 4–7 percent reporting probable PTSD.[21] Although the exact reasons for the heightened likelihood of such conditions in the contractor population are unknown, one hypothesis seemingly supported by existing data is that the private military industry stigmatizes

---

[18] Dunigan et al., 2013.

[19] Dunigan et al., 2013.

[20] Institute of Medicine, *Returning Home from Iraq and Afghanistan: Assessment of Readjustment Needs of Veterans, Service Members, and Their Families*, Washington, D.C.: National Academies Press, 2013.

[21] Dunigan et al., 2013.

seeking treatment and that mental health treatment and long-term insurance are not readily available to contractors in the industry.[22]

The lack of long-term support for deployment-related mental and physical health problems acquired while working on contract is a sensitive and volatile topic among personnel working on the Western side of the industry, and it is worthy of further exploration with regard to Russian private military contractors. Indeed, in the United States, there has been extensive media reporting on injured contractors waiting for years for approval of Defense Base Act insurance claims, and in a number of cases—at least anecdotally—such claims are outright denied.[23]

There are preliminary indications that Russian contractor personnel similarly suffer from physical and mental stress as a result of contract deployments. Lower-ranking Russian contractor personnel have claimed that they arrived in Syria to find the standards far worse than advertised, with harsh living conditions, poor food, and insufficient weaponry. The stress of this operating environment is likely compounded by the illegal status of the private military industry in Russia, which essentially carries with it a constant threat of being arrested and imprisoned for performing this work.

Those who complain about any of these conditions are reportedly afforded no reprieve and offered no way out of the country in which they are operating until their contract term has been completed. Meanwhile, higher-ranking contractors in the corporate structure of a given firm reportedly receive better treatment and even a percentage of profits.[24] Some supporters, including Yevgeny Shabaev, who has filed a

---

[22] Dunigan et al., 2013.

[23] T. Christian Miller, "AIG Faces Inquiry over Medical Care for U.S. Contractors," ProPublica, April 22, 2009a; T. Christian Miller, "Congressional Hearing: Officials Admit Major Flaws in Program to Aid Wounded War-Zone Workers," ProPublica, June 19, 2009b; T. Christian Miller, "The Other Victims of Battlefield Stress; Defense Contractors' Mental Health Neglected," ProPublica, February 26, 2010a; T. Christian Miller, "This Year, Contractor Deaths Exceed Military Ones in Iraq and Afghanistan," ProPublica, September 23, 2010b; T. Christian Miller, "Foreign Workers for U.S. Are Casualties Twice Over," ProPublica, June 19, 2009c; T. Christian Miller and Doug Smith, "Injured Civilians Battle to Get Care," *Los Angeles Times*, April 17, 2009.

[24] Giglio, 2019.

petition on Russian contractors' behalf with the International Criminal Court, claim that many Wagner members have returned home with PTSD and other medical issues that go unaddressed.[25] Basic treatment is apparently afforded to these personnel only when they are suffering from immediate battlefield wounds, but—as in the rest of the global private military industry—they receive no long-term treatment or medical follow-up.[26]

It is not clear how well known the high rates of PTSD and limited support are among the broader Russian population. Any increase in publicity about the challenges that PMC personnel face could lead to recruitment and retention challenges. Indeed, such health issues—widely broadcast across the country and among those demographics from which PMCs hire—could affect recruitment over time.

Economics

Economics in the military will-to-fight model can be tied to both oneself and one's family. This factor includes several drivers that can directly affect one's will to fight: (1) the need for subsistence, (2) the need for socioeconomic advancement, and (3) a motivation to earn money and improve one's quality of life.[27] As alluded to earlier with regard to both the definition of *mercenary* and the identity of private military actors, economic motivations and overall incentives for a lucrative career are strong. Most accounts paint a picture of self-interested contractors working for Russian PMCs, with patriotism or loyalty to any state being less of a motivator than what is typically observed among Western contractors. After 2014, Russia experienced a visible economic downturn, with both living standards and real wages rapidly falling. Reports indicate that the typical recruit between 2015 and 2019 was a middle-aged Russian man (35–50 years old) with a military background and a family or dependents to support.[28]

---

[25] Maria Tsvetkova, "Russian Military Veterans Seek ICC Investigation of Mercenary Deployments," Reuters, November 9, 2018.

[26] Giglio, 2019.

[27] Connable et al., 2018, p. 54.

[28] Sukhankin, 2018b.

At the height of Operation Iraqi Freedom and Operation Enduring Freedom in Afghanistan, contractors in the Western private military industry were able to make nearly a soldier's annual salary in just one month. Two contractor interviewees who served in Afghanistan in 2002 and 2003 (with one returning for one month in late 2004) noted that they were making approximately $1,000 per day while deployed, working as PMC team leaders.[29] Such pay was extreme even for among Western firms at the time and has abated somewhat. It is important to note that local nationals and third-country nationals (TCNs) who work for Western PMCs are paid substantially less than their Western-born counterparts. Wages for these personnel are approximately one-eighth to one-fifteenth of those paid to Westerners.[30]

Data on funding and wages for Russian private military actors is less reliable and murkier, but media reports indicate that pay for contractors who work for Russian firms varies based on the deployment in question, level of seniority, and operational position in the field. Available data do not capture wages for various services performed by Russian contractors, but the type of service performed is also likely a relevant factor dictating one's pay. Prior to deploying to Ukraine or Syria in the period between 2015 and 2019, Wagner personnel could expect to receive 80,000 rubles ($1,300) per month during preparations at Molkino. In Ukraine, contractor personnel were reportedly paid 20,000 rubles ($1,900) monthly, along with 180,000 rubles ($2,900) monthly for "installing order" on the territory of the "Luhansk People's Republic," the occupied, separatist portion of Ukraine's Luhansk region. In addition, personnel were guaranteed 60,000 rubles ($960) per week while serving in action in Ukraine. Compensation to the family of a contractor killed on one of these deployments varied from 2 million to 3 million rubles ($32,000–$48,000). Notably, the "insur-

[29] Dunigan, 2011, citing interviews with former private military contractor personnel, April 2007.

[30] Amanda Chisholm, "Marketing the Gurkha Security Package: Colonial Histories and Neoliberal Economies of Private Security," *Security Dialogue*, Vol. 45, No. 4, August 2014, p. 354; see also Amanda Chisholm, "The Silenced and Indispensable: Gurkhas in Private Military Security Companies," *International Feminist Journal of Politics*, Vol. 16, No. 1, 2014.

gents" from the Donetsk and Luhansk People's Republics were making significantly less: approximately 15,000 rubles ($240) per month.[31]

From 2015 to 2016, the average salary earned by Wagner employees in Syria may have reached 240,000 rubles ($3,800) per month; if a deployment lasted an entire year, total pay would be the equivalent of $45,600. Russian sources suggest that monthly wages in early 2017—the height of the Russian campaign in Syria—may have been as high as 500,000 rubles ($8,000), or the equivalent of $96,000 annually. However, other sources suggest that salaries were in the range of 150,000–300,000 rubles ($2,300–$4,800) per month during this period.[32] Family compensation for a death in combat was reportedly up to 5 million rubles ($80,000), which is equal to the standard compensation for the death of a Russian soldier.[33]

Notably, these figures are significantly lower than the pay offered to Western expatriates who perform security services for Western PMCs. They are nonetheless dramatically higher than the average monthly salary in Russia, which was, as of March 2020, 50,926 rubles per month (approximately USD $740, or an annual salary equivalent to $8,880).[34]

Perhaps more importantly, the reported wages offered by Russian PMCs are not significantly lower than those paid by U.S. firms, such as KBR, Fluor, and DynCorp, to Eastern European logistical support contractors in the Balkans conflicts in the mid-1990s and in Iraq in more recent years. Indeed, the U.S. Army's Logistics Civil Augmentation Program (LOGCAP), which provides the vast majority of logistical support for the Army worldwide, specifically directs its prime contractors to bring TCN salaries into line with the prevailing

---

[31] Sukhankin, 2018b.

[32] Sukhankin, 2018b; Ray Finch, "Private Russian Soldiers in Syria," *OE Watch*, Vol. 6, No. 10, October 2016. These figures align with those cited in an interview with a former Wagner contractor published in the Russian newspaper *Moskovsky Komsomolets*, who reported that Russian mercenaries are paid approximately $2,600 a month, while senior personnel are paid more than $4,000 per month. See Gurcan, 2019.

[33] Sukhankin, 2018b.

[34] Trading Economics, "Russia Average Monthly Wages," data for March 2020.

wages of their home countries.[35] In practice, this has meant that the salaries of Western PMC personnel from the same countries where Russian PMCs recruit—Bosnia, Kosovo, and elsewhere in Eastern Europe—are the same or less than the reported salaries offered to Wagner fighters in Syria in recent years. Adam Moore outlines this dynamic in his book on the evolution of Bosnian TCN pay in Iraq:

> DynCorp, for instance, classified its employees according to four categories: 1) Expats (Americans), 2) Foreign National United Kingdom (FNUK), 3) Foreign National European (FNE), and 4) Foreign National Asian (FNA). Pay and privileges were roughly equivalent for expats and FNUK employees. My interviews suggest that DynCorp paid FNE workers (which were primarily from Bosnia, Macedonia, and Kosovo) less than KBR, with salaries for most positions between $30,000 and $50,000 [annually].[36]

Critical assessment of the incentives and pay structure for personnel working for Russian private military actors may highlight ways in which the U.S. military can manipulate the labor market for these Russian firms. It may be worthwhile for future research on this topic to probe the possibility of luring Russian nationals and other citizens from Eastern European countries to work for Western PMCs employed primarily by U.S. government organizations and allied clients. To do this, contract mechanisms, such as LOGCAP, would need to be revised to ensure that the United States offers adequate wages and other career incentives to attract contractor personnel who might otherwise work for Russian PMCs. Although directly hiring Russian nationals for such positions would likely spark legitimate security concerns, shifting current practices among U.S. firms to reduce inequalities in pay between TCN contractors with Eastern European and Asian citizenship and their U.S. and Western counterparts could assist in channeling third-country labor toward the U.S. side of the industry and away from Russian PMCs. Such a strategy would be most useful if targeted specifically at the demo-

---

[35] Adam Moore, *Empire's Labor: The Global Army That Supports U.S. Wars*, Ithaca, N.Y.: Cornell University Press, 2019, p. 57.

[36] Moore, 2019, p. 57.

graphic most likely to find Russian PMC employment to be an attractive option: middle-aged military veterans with families or other financial commitments who hail from countries targeted for recruitment.

Team-Level Factors
Cohesion

Cohesion in the military will-to-fight model includes *task cohesion* and *social cohesion*, both operating at the unit level. *Task cohesion* is a commitment to collective goals. It defines units or teams composed of "members who share a common goal and who are motivated to coordinate their efforts as a team to achieve that goal."[37] *Social cohesion*, meanwhile, "is bonding based on friendship, trust, or other aspects of interpersonal relationships," formed through, for example, "through shared experience and hardship." In the model, "Social cohesion in the standard model of military group cohesion includes both horizontal (peer) and vertical (leader) bonds."[38]

In the case of private military actors, we were particularly interested in task cohesion, not only among the components of a private military team itself but also between contractors and the military forces they operate alongside in the field. Prior research has found that successful PMC-military coordination in the field allows the entire force to be more responsive to its own needs and capabilities, as well as to external conditions, increasing its level of integration and military effectiveness.

Stated more directly, high levels of task cohesion between private military actors and their state military counterparts can increase mili-

---

[37] Robert J. MacCoun, "What Is Known About Unit Cohesion and Military Performance," in Bernard Rostker, Scott A. Harris, James P. Kahan, Erik J. Frinking, C. Neil Fulcher, Lawrence M. Hanser, Paul Koegel, John D. Winkler, Brent A. Boultinghouse, Joanna Heilbrunn, Janet Lever, Robert J. MacCoun, Peter Tiemeyer, Gail L. Zellman, Sandra H. Berry, Jennifer Hawes-Dawson, Samantha Ravich, Steven L. Schlossman, Timothy Haggarty, Tanjam Jacobson, Ancella Livers, Sherie Mershon, Andrew Cornell, Mark A. Schuster, David E. Kanouse, Raynard Kington, Mark Litwin, Conrad Peter Schmidt, Carl H. Builder, Peter Jacobson, Stephen A. Saltzburg, Roger Allen Brown, William Fedorochko, Marilyn Fisher Freemon, John F. Peterson, and James A. Dewar, *Sexual Orientation and US Military Personnel Policy: Options and Assessment*, Santa Monica, Calif.: RAND Corporation, MR-323-OSD, 1993, p. 291.

[38] Connable et al., 2018, p. 65.

tary effectiveness by increasing will to fight at the team level. In Operation Iraqi Freedom and Operation Enduring Freedom in Afghanistan, particularly in the early years of both conflicts, much of the coordination between private military contractors and supposedly allied military forces was ad hoc. When coordination problems occurred, they came with many interrelated problems that influenced military effectiveness, including friendly fire incidents between PSC and military personnel (so-called blue-on-white incidents), resentment over differences between PMC and military pay, the military's lack of knowledge regarding PMCs' presence in their areas of responsibility, and PMCs' often-negative impact on local civilians' perceptions of the entire military operation.[39]

In any situation of private military contractor employment, it is critical to determine whether and to what extent contractors will be operating in the field alongside a state's military forces. At issue is not only C2 complexity generated by the presence of a variety of force types in one area of responsibility but also the conceivable levels of cohesion versus resentment between these forces. As Ryan Kelty notes,

> With the increase in civilian contracting, especially contractors who work alongside soldiers and perform similar (or at least comparable) duties, highly salient aspects of one's job are likely to become points of social comparison between service members and the civilian contractors with whom they work. For example, social comparisons could be expected, in particular, with regard to pay, benefits, autonomy, level or risk for injury and death, and impact of one's employment on one's family.[40]

Military personnel have indicated several reasons for their resentment of contractors in both the Iraq and Afghanistan theaters, including perceived differences in pay and living conditions and their perception of contractors' disregard for local civilians and respected norms. Some military personnel have reported that contractors' "cowboy" tac-

---

[39] Dunigan, 2011, chapt. 3.

[40] Ryan Kelty, "Citizen Soldiers and Civilian Contractors: Military Outsourcing, Unit Cohesion, and Retention Attitudes," Chestertown, Md.: Washington College, 2011, p. 5.

tics make their own jobs more difficult.[41] Other surveyed U.S. military personnel reported concerns about PMC employment options having a negative impact on military retention, particularly in the special operations forces communities.[42] Kelty's analysis of survey data from U.S. Army personnel returning from overseas deployments showed a direct correlation between soldiers' job satisfaction and their attitudes toward contractors: "The more positively soldiers view contractors, the more satisfied they are with their job."[43]

Cohesion between military and contractor populations is likely to be most challenging when appropriate structures are not in place to facilitate their coordination, including streamlined communications and C2 structures. In the case of the Russian private military industry, cohesion between the military and contractor populations may be less of an issue than it is in the Western side of the industry, as it appears that such firms are closer to state-sanctioned auxiliaries, as discussed in Chapter Two. Additionally, the Wagner Group appears to maintain a clear and well-developed C2 system, following a template drawn from the structure of the Russian armed forces—this may enable their coordination with parallel state military structures.[44] Yet, this dynamic of cohesion between private and public forces—especially when co-deployed alongside one another in a particular theater—is worth watching carefully because it has a historical tendency to be problematic in other cases of military privatization and other PMCs. In these cases, it may be worthwhile to explore how U.S. forces might sow disorder and resentment between Russian private military contractors and Russian military forces. This could manifest tactical, operational, and

---

[41] Dunigan, 2011, pp. 76–85; Cotton et al., 2010.

[42] Cotton et al., 2010; Christopher Spearin, "Special Operations Forces a Strategic Resource: Public and Private Divides," *Parameters*, Vol. 36, No. 4, Winter 2006–2007.

[43] Kelty, 2011, pp. 8–9.

[44] Wagner's C2 structure includes an upper level consisting of the commander-in-chief and a managing director and a middle level consisting of an administrative group, the general staff, and the control group. Various subunits are responsible for firearm training, engineer training, tank and infantry fighting vehicle crews, tactical training, and artillery and anti-air defense. It has been argued that this structure allows Wagner to carry out offensive missions or operations usually performed by the regular armed forces. See Sukhankin, 2018b.

strategic inefficiencies among Russian forces and could be a fruitful point of vulnerability to leverage in future conflicts.

Company/Organizational-Level Factors
Control
Control is addressed at both the unit and organizational levels in the military will-to-fight model, analogous to the team and company levels in the private military sphere. At both the unit and organization levels, control is defined as follows:

> This is the method of obtaining obedience to orders and pursuit of mission objectives. Control relies on a mix of coercion and persuasion, and it is reflected in discipline. Coercion is a set of unit-imposed motivations that involve fear, compulsion, punishment, and external threats to elicit obedience; these can include cultural norms that result in social punishments, in addition to authoritarian physical threats. Persuasion is encouragement to perform the formal and informal standards of behavior, and can include rewards, discussion, ideological conditioning, and intraunit competition. Discipline reflects the cultural approach to control and defines the relationships between leaders and soldiers.[45]

In the unit and organizational contexts, *control* is defined similarly but measured differently; most critically, unit leaders are understood to seek to mirror organizational standards, and organizational control is less likely to change over the course of a single battle or short series of battles.[46] Control reflects that individual will to fight may not be inherently strong, but unit and organizational-level coercion are sufficiently strong that, on the surface, the will to fight of the entire unit or organization appears to be quite robust. The implication is that will to fight may be vulnerable if targeted accordingly, but there is risk in such targeting due to unit or organizational-level oversight.

---

[45] Connable et al., 2018, p. 76.

[46] Connable et al., 2018, p. 76.

In the private military industry, control is indeed also relevant at the team (unit) and company (organizational) levels, with extensive literature on the inability of team leaders or company management to keep unwilling contractors in the field if they wish to abandon their posts—at least on the Western side of the industry.[47] This speculation is usually couched in terms of the strategic, operational, and tactical risks to the state in replacing military forces with contractors in the field, but there have also been reports of less reputable companies engaging in human trafficking of TCN contractors. Such activities typically involve recruiting personnel in third countries with promises of lucrative and easy work, then holding their passports once they arrive in the theater of conflict until they have worked through the duration of their contract.[48] Other types of control reported in the Western private military industry include team leaders assigning TCNs to the worst shifts and even beating local nationals who—in line with their assigned guard duties—refuse team leaders' entry to officially restricted areas.[49]

Interestingly, the "control" activities of Russian PMC teams and corporate leadership align neatly with such activities on the Western side of the industry. One distinction is that the private military indus-

---

[47] Deborah Avant, "The Privatization of Security: Lessons from Iraq," *Orbis*, Vol. 50, No. 2, Spring 2006; Jennifer K. Elsea, Moshe Schwartz, Kennon H. Nakamura, *Private Security Contractors in Iraq: Background, Legal Status, and Other Issues*, Washington, D.C.: Congressional Research Service, RL32419, August 25, 2008; U.S. General Accounting Office, *Military Operations Contractors Provide Vital Services to Deployed Forces but Are Not Adequately Addressed in DoD Plans*, Washington, D.C., GAO-03-695, June 2003; William G. Holt II, *Battlefield Contractors: Operational Risk and System Support Contractors*, Newport, R.I.: Naval War College, October 27, 2010; Kim M. Nelson, *Contractors on the Battlefield: Force Multipliers or Force Dividers?* Maxwell Air Force Base, Ala.: Air Command and Staff College, April 2000; Linda Robinson, "America's Secret Armies: A Swarm of Private Contractors Bedevils the U.S. Military," *U.S. News and World Report*, November 4, 2002; Anthony K. Whitson, *Logistical Contractors on the Peacekeeping (PKO) Battlefield: A Guide for the Operational Commander*, Newport, R.I.: Naval War College, February 2001.

[48] Corporate confiscation of TCNs' passports was reportedly occurring as recently as 2018 in Iraq; several employees of Reston, Virginia–based Sallyport Global reported that the company their passports were taken when they landed in country. See Zack Kopplin and Irvin McCullough, "U.S. Paid $1B to Contractor Accused of Bigotry at Iraq Air Base," *Daily Beast*, September 18, 2018.

[49] Kopplin and McCullough, 2018.

try is illegal in Russia, as noted. Marten and other analysts have speculated that such illegality is a mechanism for Putin or the FSB to control
private military actors. If they are operating illegally, their loyalty may
be ensured through threats of imprisonment at any time.[50] The Russian state has indeed leveraged this power: As *Foreign Policy* reported,
upon returning from "an abortive attempt to regain control of oil fields
in Syria's eastern province of Deir ez-Zor" in 2013, an entire contin-
gent of 267 Russian contractors working for a Hong Kong–based company, Slavonic Corps, was "taken into temporary custody by waiting
FSB agents who confiscated their SIM cards, electronic media, and
passports and began interrogating them individually." Slavonic Corps
was allegedly hired by the Russian PMC Moran under a contract with
the Syrian government. Two members of Moran's leadership team were
also arrested and faced prison time.[51]

Other aspects of Russian private military deployments share
striking similarities with the control dynamics seen in PMCs' treatment
of TCNs on the Western side of the industry. Russian investigative
journalists found that, prior to the aborted mission and mass
detainment of Moran's Slavonic Corps subcontractors, Slavonic Corps
had been recruiting former Russian soldiers with combat experience to
guard "energy facilities" in exotic locales for the promise of $4,000 per
month, at Moran's direction:

> [R]ecruits were invited to Moscow, where they were told, in
> Moran's offices, that they'd be subcontracted to Syria with
> Slavonic Corps. . . . Right away, people signed a contract that
> included a will to bury their remains in their homeland or, if that
> proved impossible, in the nation where they died, and then be
> reburied in Russia. . . . They were given assault rifles, machine
> guns, and grenade launchers as well as other Soviet-era hardware,
> some of it 70 years old.

According to one unnamed Slavonic Corps mercenary:

---

[50] Marten, 2019. On the benefits to the Russian state of maintaining the industry's legal
opacity, see Borshchevskaya, 2019.

[51] Weiss, 2013.

"When they spoke to us in Russia, they explained that we were going on a contract with the Syrian government; they convinced us that everything was legal and in order. Like, our government and the FSB were on board and involved in the project. When we arrived there, it turned out that we were sent as gladiators, under a contract with some Syrian or other, who may or may not have a relationship with the government. . . . That meant that we were the private army of a local kingpin. But there was no turning back. As they said, a return ticket costs money, and we'll work it off, whether we like it or not."[52]

Available information indicates that some individual contractor personnel working for Russian PMCs may be fighting under coercion and could be vulnerable to efforts to turn their loyalties. Weak loyalty and resulting loss of personnel could trigger downstream human capital issues in the Russian private military industry. However, this possibility should be viewed with caution; there is similarly some countervailing evidence that the idea of joining Wagner or other Russian PMCs has gained in popularity and that potential recruits will, in the near term, be plentiful. As Candace Rondeaux noted in a 2020 Defense One podcast episode,

[I]f you look at VKontakte, which is the Russian version of Facebook, these groups have grown in popularity. The sort of mysticism around [them] . . . has grown exponentially since the start of the Ukraine war, certainly.[53]

Further exploration of possible fruitful approaches to both exploit the interests of such personnel and to educate them regarding potential brutality and poor living and working conditions in the ranks of a privatized deployment is needed and would be a useful direction for future research.

---

[52] Weiss, 2013.

[53] Defense One Radio, "Wagner and Russian Private Military Contractors," podcast episode, January 15, 2020.

State- and Societal-Level Factors
Support

Support is relevant at both the state and societal levels in the military will-to-fight model. State support is defined as the extent to which states deliver "equipment, weapons, vehicles, medical supplies, and so on through the organization to the unit and the individual." The military model adds, "Sufficient and timely material support is important for the sustainment of military operations, and therefore for sustainment of will to fight."[54] Societal support, on the other hand, takes many forms, the most common being "popular support, material support, and recruiting support."[55] Most importantly, the military will-to-fight model highlights the *consistency* and *efficiency* of societal support as critical subfactors for assessing support's impact on will to fight. Indeed, a lack of either state or societal support can weaken will to fight.

State support of private military actors is, in some ways, superfluous. States frequently contract with PMCs to increase flexibility and to avoid having to provide services directly. Indeed, a large proportion of U.S. contracting dollars are devoted to logistical support, weapon maintenance and upkeep, and transportation contracts, such as LOGCAP, capped for its fifth iteration in LOGCAP V at $82 billion over ten years.[56] In such cases, the state is effectively contracting out its support function to private entities.

Yet, it is relevant to note that, in U.S. defense policy, contractors are officially denoted as a key component of the tripartite "total force," which is composed of military, DoD civilians, and DoD-hired contractors.[57] Because contractors constitute an official arm of the U.S. defense structure, DoD expects to support those employed on DoD contracts, either organically or through the use of other contractors.

---

[54] Connable et al., 2018, p. 98.

[55] Connable et al., 2018, p. 106.

[56] U.S. Army Sustainment Command, Public Affairs, "LOGCAP V Performance Contractors Selected," April 15, 2019.

[57] U.S. Code, Title 10, Subtitle A, Chapter 3, Section 129a, General Policy for Total Force Management; U.S. Department of Defense Instruction 1100.22, *Policy and Procedures for Determining Workforce Mix*, Washington, D.C., incorporating change 1, December 1, 2017.

Often, specific types of support to be provided by the state client are written into contract terms.

Russian private military actors appear to receive some comparable levels of state support. As noted, wounded Wagner Group contractors have been airlifted from Russian military bases in Syria to recover at Russian hospitals; they also share training sites with Russian military bases. Yet, due to PMCs' illegal status, state support wavers at times. For instance, as Slavonic Corps personnel retreated from the battlefield at Deir ez-Zor, other teams of Russian private military actors had to call in helicopter teams to evacuate the wounded from the battlefield; Russian state forces did not do so, for whatever reason.[58] Wavering state linkages to the industry decrease predictability in how Russia will utilize such forces, how well private military actors will be resourced and supported, and how they will behave.

Societal support, meanwhile, is an interesting and apparently Janus-faced factor with regard to military privatization in both the West and in Russia. Indeed, its most critical reflection is that societal ignorance—or lack of societal attention—drives the utilization of private military actors. PMC employment has an ability to reduce transparency and accountability to democratic processes and, by extension, to popular support. There is the potential for negative public opinion when it is revealed that PMC personnel are engaging in activities that would ordinarily be performed by state military personnel or when they participate in covert activities that are legally or politically off limits for state military forces.[59]

In both the Western and Russian cases, so-called "back-door deployments" of contractors—designed to obviate any formal counting of a particular state's boots on the ground—provide a state with plausible deniability, both to foreign and domestic actors, about activities in a given area. One manifestation of the utility of PMC-derived plausible deniability for the state is the absence of societal attention to casualty counts for contractor personnel. For instance, while it has become fairly common knowledge that private military actors have

---

[58] Marten, 2019.

[59] Dunigan, 2011, chapt. 4.

accounted for most of the losses on the Russian side of the ground war in Syria, information on the number of contractor deaths varies. In 2016, a Russian Ministry of Defence official insisted that only 27 "private soldiers" had been killed in Syria, while another account placed the number at 100 or more.[60] In an oft-cited February 2018 battle in Deir ez-Zor between U.S.-backed Syrian Defense Forces and Russian private military actors, casualty estimates varied but were as high as 600 deaths among the Russian private military forces.[61] Moreover, relatives of those slain tend to refuse to talk, and Wagner personnel claim that nondisclosure of the terms of working for a PMC is a condition of their family receiving compensation.[62]

Due to the lack of attention to contractor casualties, popular support for a state's involvement in particular conflicts may be inflated beyond what would be seen if they were military deployments and associated military casualties. The presence of politically active "mothers' groups" in Russia may help to spread information on contractor casualties, but the extent of their influence remains to be seen, and they too often have incomplete information regarding contractor casualties.[63]

Tenuous societal support due to a lack of information allows the state to utilize contractors with plausible deniability, hidden from domestic and foreign observers. To exploit this factor, U.S. forces may consider methods of broadly messaging information about Russian involvement in foreign conflicts, including the use of Russian military veterans, to the Russian public, as well as information on the casualties inflicted thus far, with the intent of increasing public opposition and limiting Russia's ability to use PMC personnel at all.

---

[60] Finch, 2016; Konrad Bingham and James Muzyka, "Private Companies Engage in Russia's Non-Linear Warfare," *Jane's Intelligence Review,* January 29, 2018.

[61] Rondeaux, 2019, p. 10.

[62] Finch, 2016; Maria Tsvetkova and Anton Zverev, "Ghost Soldiers: The Russians Secretly Dying for the Kremlin in Syria," Reuters, November 3, 2016.

[63] Paul A. Goble, "Russian Soldiers' Mothers Group Helping 7,000 Soldiers and Family Members Every Year," *Euromaidan Press,* October 4, 2014; Terrence McCoy, "What Does Russia Tell the Mothers of Soldiers Killed in Ukraine? Not Much," *Washington Post,* August 29, 2014.

Linking Model Factors to Strategies to Counter Russian Private Military Actors

Better understanding of the motivations of a new ground force adversary confronted by the United States in numerous theaters and in notably large numbers in Syria will empower U.S. forces and leadership to develop an effective strategy to counter it. Indeed, for USASOC, considering Russian private military actors' motivations as they align with or diverge from the military will-to-fight model in the Syrian theater and elsewhere could greatly strengthen U.S. tactical, operational, and strategic positions against such forces. Chapter Four expands on these findings and offers specific suggestions for cognitive maneuver activities that may be pursued against Russian private military actors in Syria and beyond.

Conclusions, Recommendations, and Next Steps

The primary objectives of this research were to use RAND's military will-to-fight model as a lens to preliminarily analyze Russian private military activity in Syria and elsewhere to enable USASOC and other U.S. military and government entities to better assess (1) what motivates and demotivates Russian private military contractors and the companies that hire them to fight, (2) what motivates and demotivates the Russian state government to utilize private military actors in Syria, and (3) what USASOC and other U.S. military and government entities can do to influence such activities.

As noted in Chapter One, we designed this research to meet these objectives by answering three interrelated research questions:

1. Who are the relevant actors in the Russian private military sphere to consider when assessing Russian private forces' will to fight?
2. What factors are most relevant to Russian private military actors' will to fight?
3. How do Russian private military actors compare with their current and historical Western counterparts, and what lessons can be drawn from these comparative cases to inform U.S. opportunities to defeat adversary-employed private military actors?

This chapter presents our conclusions and recommendations as they relate to these research questions.

Who Are the Relevant Actors in the Russian Private Military Sphere?

Founded by former GRU Spetsnaz commander Dmitry Utkin in 2014, the Wagner Group is the most high-profile of Russia's private military actors. When Moscow launched its military intervention in Syria in fall 2015, Wagner deployed more than 2,000 personnel there.[1] Wagner contractors also took part in the 2014 annexation of Crimea and have fought in Ukraine, Sudan, the Central African Republic, Madagascar, Libya, and Mozambique.[2] Other Russian private military actors have reportedly been active as far back as the late 1990s in Iraq, Afghanistan, Ukraine, Syria, Libya, Chechnya, Tajikistan, Yemen, and Burundi. Such actors include Cossacks, Anti-Terror Orel, the Slavonic Corps, Moran Security Group, RSB Group, E.N.O.T. Corps, MAR, DOBRANDR, Turan, Centre R, ATK Group, Tigr Top-Rent Security, and Patriot.

What Factors Are Most Relevant to Russian Private Military Actors' Will to Fight?

Because the private military industry is transnational and influenced by business, government, military, and transnational society interests, we recommend modifications to the military will-to-fight model to account for various motivations of industry actors. We defined a private military will-to-fight model comprising factors at the individual level, the contractor operator team level, the PMC/organizational level, the state level, and the societal level. Spanning these five levels, we identified five factors as particularly important for understanding the will to fight of private military actors—specifically, Russian private military actors: *identity, economics, cohesion, control,* and *support,* with the additional factor of *individual well-being.*

---

[1]   Gurcan, 2017.

[2]   Browne, 2019; Lister, Shukla, and Ward, 2019; Flanagan, 2019; Marten, 2019.

How Do Russian Private Military Actors Compare with Their Current and Historical Western Counterparts?

The activities of Russian private military actors since the late 1990s in Iraq, Afghanistan, Ukraine, Syria, Libya, Chechnya, Tajikistan, Yemen, Burundi, Sudan, the Central African Republic, Madagascar, and Syria, as well as media speculation of Wagner activity in Libya and Mozambique, reveal that Russian private military actors and their relationships to the Russian state and society differ in some ways from historical cases of military privatization. However, in other ways, Russia's use of private military actors bears striking similarities to private military activity by the United States, United Kingdom, and South Africa, among other countries.

First and foremost, Russian private military actors are reminiscent of auxiliaries and, therefore, closer to mercenaries, than Western private military actors. A fine-grained, preliminary view of Russian private military actors' characteristics and motivations in line with each of the private military will-to-fight model factors provides further comparative insight.[3]

Observations

Individual Factors
Identity
The individual identities of contractor personnel vary, and the impact of identity on one's will to fight is therefore variable. Although it is difficult to definitively confirm the various components of the identity of Russian private military actors operating in Syria between 2015 and 2019, we do know that they are typically Eastern European, not necessarily patriotic, and likely had a background in military or intelligence skill sets that they were seeking to apply to lucrative work beyond the military.

---

[3] Note that this analysis represents an initial cut at identifying the will-to-fight factors relevant to the private military sphere; further exploration would extend these analyses through an in-depth coding of each factor using the will-to-fight tool.

Individual Well-Being

Challenges to individual well-being may decrease will to fight, as well as effective occupational functioning while performing tasks in theater. Anecdotal reports indicate that Russian contractors have returned home from Syrian deployments with PTSD and other physical and mental health problems that tend to go unaddressed over the long term. Although these outcomes do not diverge from the industry norm, according to transnational studies of private military contractors' health and well-being, this finding presents a potentially exploitable vulnerability within this population.

Economics

Economic factors in the military will-to-fight model can be associated with the self or one's family and include drivers that directly affect an individual's will to fight: (1) the need for subsistence, (2) the need for socioeconomic advancement, and (3) the motivation to earn money and improve quality of life. Compiled data from media reports indicate that pay rates for Russian private military actors—even at the more senior operational levels—are significantly lower than for Western contractors who provide security services in theaters of conflict under the auspices of Western PMCs. However, the pay offered to contractors who work for Russian private military actors was significantly higher than the average monthly salary in Russia as of early 2020 and was, in some cases, higher than what U.S. prime contractors paid Eastern European contractors in Iraq in the early and mid-2000s.

Team Factor: Cohesion

High levels of task cohesion between private military actors and their state military counterparts can increase military effectiveness by positively influencing will to fight at the team level. Notably, at least one currently active Russian PMC, the Wagner Group, appears to maintain a clear and well-developed C2 system following a template drawn from the structure of the Russian armed forces. Such a structured C2 approach may assist in improving task cohesion between contractors and allied military forces they deploy alongside.

Company and Organizational Factor: Control

If unit and organizational-level coercion are sufficiently strong, on the surface, the will to fight of the entire unit or organization would appear to be quite robust. *Control*, therefore, may obscure vulnerability in individual will to fight that may be targeted accordingly, but there is risk in such targeting due to unit or organizational oversight.

Unlike the situation in many Western markets for privatized forces, the private military industry is illegal in Russia. Some speculate that this intentional illegality is a mechanism for Putin or the FSB to control private military actors and ensure their loyalty. Other mechanisms of both unit and organizational control appear to include recruiting personnel with promises of lucrative and easy work, then holding their passports until their contract has been fulfilled.

State and Societal Factor: Support

A lack of state or societal support can weaken will to fight. Russian private military actors appear to receive comparable levels of state support as their Western counterparts. For example, wounded contractors are treated in Russian hospitals and share training sites with Russian military bases. Yet, due to the industry's illegal status in Russia, state support wavers at times. Societal support is more tenuous, and it is the *absence* of societal awareness and hence support that seems to enable Russia's use of private military actors and thus may be a vulnerability in these forces' will to fight. Indeed, intentional obfuscation regarding contractor casualty counts has led to a dearth of Russian popular attention to the use of contractors, which effectively equates to a public "nod" to these deployments from Russian society.

Historical Lessons Learned: What Are the Best Options for Countering Adversary-Employed Private Military Actors in Syria and Beyond?

Based on the foregoing analyses and conclusions, we recommend that USASOC and the broader U.S. government pursue three lines of effort to exploit vulnerabilities associated with Russia's use of private military actors in Syria. Because the private military industry is transnational and many of the same traits and practices characterize these actors and their roles across operational theaters, these lines of effort will similarly apply to areas of responsibility beyond Syria. Many of these recommendations center on messaging activities that are likely to be conducted by USASOC psychological operations forces; however, all USASOC components should look for opportunities to exploit these vulnerabilities within their own mission sets.

Table 4.1 summarizes our recommendations, broken down by will-to-fight model level and factor.

Individual and Company/Organizational Levels: Exploit Vulnerabilities in the Recruitment and Retention of Promising Contractor Personnel

Analyses via the lenses of the *identity, economics, individual well-being,* and *control* factors provide insight into conceivably fruitful cognitive maneuver activities for USASOC to pursue at the individual and company/organizational levels. The preliminary evidence indicates that Russian contractor personnel tend to select this type of work for self-interested or clientelistic reasons and are often not treated well by

Table 4.1
Factor-Based Analysis of Russian Case: Summary of Recommendations

Level	Recommendation
Individual, company, and organizational	Exploit vulnerabilities in recruitment and retention of contractor personnel and in their loyalty and commitment to the Russian state and Russian PMCs.
	Broadcast warnings to potential recruits about the coercive nature of contracts, disparities in pay and living conditions between contractor ranks, and mental and physical health risks and difficulty of accessing treatment.
Team	Identify and exploit opportunities to sow disorder or exacerbate tensions between Russian private military actors and Russian military forces.
State and societal	Create societal backlash to Russia's use of contractors by publicly disseminating information about contractors' veteran status and treatment and data on contractor casualties.

the Russian government. Indeed, in some cases, it appears that they are victims of outright exploitation by the state or the companies they work for. Some Russian contractor personnel may be fighting under PMC coercion and could be vulnerable to efforts to turn their loyalties. These individuals may therefore be moderately vulnerable and their loyalties highly malleable. It follows that efforts to weaken their loyalty and commitment may prove fruitful.

Options for exploiting such vulnerabilities could include overt messaging efforts through social media and other venues to highlight the inequities in pay and living conditions between operational contractors on the ground and individuals higher in the ranks of the PMC corporate structure, or to highlight to the demographic of potential recruits the coercive nature of such contracts. Moreover, widely broadcasting statistics regarding contractors' deployment-related physical and mental health and the challenges in acquiring long-term treatment for these problems could affect the recruitment of both new and veteran contractors over time. Such strategies would be most effective if they specifically targeted the demographic most likely to find Russian PMC employment to be an attractive option: middle-aged military veterans with families or other financial commitments.

We urge caution in pursuing these recommendations; the data on Russian contractors' identity and motivations and on Russian PMCs' recruitment and retention tactics are scarce and of questionable reliability. There may be some contradictory evidence that contractors working in the Russian side of the industry are at least partially motivated by patriotism or that Wagner's labor pool is growing as it gains widespread global publicity. Further exploration of possible approaches to exploit the interests of such personnel is needed and could be productive. However, in the near term, the recommendations here could be an effective part of a multifaceted strategy to stymie Russian private military activity.

Team Level: Leverage Latent Discord Between Contractor and Military Populations

Analyses via the lens of the *cohesion* factor provides insight into potentially fruitful cognitive maneuver activities for USASOC to pursue at the team level. The Western side of the private military industry provides abundant examples of poor coordination and, at times, hostile or deadly interactions between contractors and supposedly allied military forces.[4] Admittedly, Western examples are not perfect analogues for the Russian case because the Russian state appears to be more directly involved in Russian PMC activity than is typical in such situations in the West, and because Russian contractors are sometimes seen as disposable "cannon fodder."[5] Nonetheless, disorder or resentment could be a fruitful point of vulnerability for Russian private military actors and an opportunity to leverage in future conflicts.

State and Societal Level: Widely Disseminate Information About Contractors' Veteran Status and Contractor Casualties to the Russian Public

Analyses via the lens of the *support* factor provide insight into possibly fruitful cognitive maneuver activities for the broader U.S. government to pursue at the state and societal levels—possibly with support from USASOC. There is evidence that contractor casualties are significantly underreported in Russia, and that contractors' families are prohibited from talking to the media if they hope to receive death compensation. Significantly, the ability to deploy additional boots on the ground beyond those counted in official military statistics has been shown to be a major incentive for states to contract with private military actors. This practice allows for plausible deniability of the state's direct involvement in such military activities. Prior research, however, indicates that when a state's population does learn of such "backdoor deployments," the reaction can be intensely negative.[6]

---

[4] Dunigan, 2011, chapt. 3; David Phinney, "Marines Jail Contractors in Iraq: Tension and Confusion Grow Amid the 'Fog of War,'" CorpWatch, June 7, 2005; Ariel Zilber, "Ex–Green Beret and Father-of-Four Who Worked as a Contractor for Lockheed Martin Dies After Being 'Pummeled into Unconsciousness by Two Marines During a Gym Altercation' While Working in Iraq," *Daily Mail*, January 8, 2019.

[5] Numerous media and scholarly reports use the term cannon fodder when describing how Wagner perceives its lowest-level forces. See, for example, Sukhankin, 2018a.

[6] Dunigan, 2011.

The U.S. government should therefore consider methods to broadly disseminate information about Russian involvement in foreign conflicts—including the use of Russian veterans in private military roles and their subsequent treatment—to the Russian public, as well as data on contractor casualties. In doing so, it would be critical to devise a well-constructed communication plan supported by clear evidence, as it is likely that such messaging would be tagged as "fake news" by Russian state media. As with the individual and company/organizational-level recommendations, we urge caution in pursuing this recommendation and advise further research into specific implementation methods.

It Is Critical for U.S. Army Special Operations Command to Understand How These Dynamics Apply in Syria and Beyond

All U.S. government agencies and military services should be concerned with Russia's increasing deployment of private military actors worldwide. Such activity allows Russia to expand its military footprint while maintaining plausible deniability and, therefore, the relative opacity of its pursuits in the competitive space short of armed conflict. The consequences of Russia's covert expansion of its ground footprint through the use of private military actors have been apparent in Syria, but this trend can be observed in Russia's operations on a global scale. To effectively engage and coordinate with other parts of the U.S. military and government, USASOC needs to be well informed about Russian private military actors' characteristics, activities, motives, and vulnerabilities. USASOC also has a unique role in combating these forces in competition short of armed conflict; indeed, Army psychological operations, civil affairs, and special operations personnel are all likely to be on the front lines, operating in near or battling such opaque forces in multidomain operations. It is critical for USASOC-aligned forces to understand Russian private military actors and their activities as they consider opportunities to exploit their vulnerabilities through cognitive maneuver.

Glossary of Terms

The following terms and definitions are drawn from the will-to-fight model as applied to military forces, but there are points of overlap in how the model applies to private military actors' will to fight.

Cohesion: Refers to *task cohesion* and *social cohesion* (also defined in this appendix) at the unit level.

Control: The method of obtaining obedience to orders and pursuit of mission objectives. Control relies on a mix of coercion and persuasion, and it is reflected in discipline. Coercion relies on a set of unit-imposed motivations that involve fear, compulsion, punishment, or external threats to elicit obedience that can invoke cultural norms and associated social punishment or physical threats. Persuasion is encouragement to conform to formal and informal standards of behavior and can include rewards, discussion, ideological conditioning, and intraunit competition. Discipline reflects the cultural approach to control and defines the relationships between leaders and personnel. Unit- and organizational-level control are defined similarly but measured differently; most critically, unit leaders are understood to seek to mirror organizational standards, and organizational control is less likely to change over the course of a single battle or a short series of battles.

Economics: Can be tied to both oneself and family and includes the need for subsistence, the desire for socioeconomic advancement, and the motivation to earn money and improve one's quality of life.

Esprit de corps: A French term generally translated as "group spirit." In military writings, it is sometimes used interchangeably with *élan* or *pride* or simply referred to as *esprit* (spirit). Esprit de corps is the fighting spirit of a unit and an ardor or eagerness to pursue a cause or task. It captures confidence in battle, prowess, and success, as well as concepts of elite membership.

Identity: Includes both social and personal characteristics or sense of belonging. The term is also frequently used in the context of a commitment to meeting expectations (e.g., about what a soldier does) or search for self-satisfaction.

Individual well-being: A person's perceived happiness, health, or prosperity. Individual well-being is influenced by both physical and mental health, as well as economic security.

Leadership: The acts of a single person in authority to direct and encourage the behaviors of personnel with the goal of accomplishing a military mission.

Social cohesion: Bonding based on friendship, trust, or other aspects of interpersonal relationships, with the essential argument being that soldiers fight because of close interpersonal bonds formed within their primary social group through shared experience and hardship. Social cohesion in the standard model of military group cohesion includes both horizontal (peer) and vertical (leader) bonds.

Societal support: The most common forms are popular support, material support, and recruiting support. The military will-to-fight model highlights the consistency and efficiency of societal support as critical subfactors for assessing changes to will to fight.

State support: The extent to which states deliver (or do not) equipment, weapons, vehicles, medical supplies, and so on through the organization to the unit and the individual. *Sufficient* and *timely* material support is important to sustain military operations and, therefore, to sustain will to fight.

Task cohesion: A commitment to collective goals.

Unit competence: Unit skills, training, and performance. Skills are resident in individuals and across units and reflect the ability to perform specific tasks. *Training* refers to the methods and capabilities used to build and maintain skills. *Performance* is the demonstration of skills.

Unit support: The sufficiency and timeliness of equipment, supplies, weapons, medical assistance, fires, food, water, and other things the unit needs to accomplish its missions.

References

Allison, Olivia, "Informal but Diverse: The Market for Exported Force from Russia and Ukraine," in Molly Dunigan and Ulrich Petersohn, eds., *The Markets for Force: Privatization of Security Across World Regions*, Philadelphia, Pa.: University of Pennsylvania Press, 2015, pp. 87–102.

American National Standards Institute and ASIS International, *Management System for Quality of Private Security Company Operations: Requirements with Guidance*, Alexandria, Va.: ASIS International, American National Standard PSC.1-2012, March 5, 2012.

Apuzzo, Matt, "Blackwater Guards Found Guilty in 2007 Iraq Killings," *New York Times*, October 22, 2014.

Astorino-Courtois, Allison, ed., *A Cognitive Capabilities Agenda: A Multi-Step Approach for Closing DoD's Cognitive Capability Gap*, Washington, D.C.: Joint Staff, Strategic Multi-Layer Assessment Office, October 2017.

Atwood, Rodney, *The Hessians: Mercenaries from Hessen-Kassel in the American Revolution*, New York: Cambridge University Press, 1980.

Avant, Deborah D., "The Privatization of Security: Lessons from Iraq," *Orbis*, Vol. 50, No. 2, Spring 2006, pp. 327–342.

Bayley, C. C., *War and Society in Renaissance Florence: The "De Militia" of Leonardo Bruni*, Toronto: University of Toronto Press, 1961.

Bingham, Konrad, and James Muzyka, "Private Companies Engage in Russia's Non-Linear Warfare," *Jane's Intelligence Review*, January 29, 2018.

Boatner, Mark Mayo III, *Encyclopedia of the American Revolution*, New York: David McKay Publications, 1969.

Borshchevskaya, Anna, *Russian Private Military Companies: Continuity and Evolution of the Model*, Philadelphia, Pa.: Foreign Policy Research Institute, December 2019. As of August 26, 2020: https://www.fpri.org/wp-content/uploads/2019/12/rfp4-borshchevskaya-final.pdf

Browne, Ryan, "Top US General Warns Russia Using Mercenaries to Access Africa's Natural Resources," CNN, February 7, 2019. As of August 26, 2020: https://www.cnn.com/2019/02/07/politics/us-russia-mercenaries-africa

Caferro, William, "Italy and the Companies of Adventure in the Fourteenth Century," *The Historian*, Vol. 58, No. 4, June 1996, pp. 795–810.

Chisholm, Amanda, "The Silenced and Indispensable: Gurkhas in Private Military Security Companies," *International Feminist Journal of Politics*, Vol. 16, No. 1, 2014, pp. 26–47.

———, "Marketing the Gurkha Security Package: Colonial Histories and Neoliberal Economies of Private Security," *Security Dialogue*, Vol. 45, No. 4, August 2014, pp. 349–372.

Connable, Ben, *Embracing the Fog of War: Assessment and Metrics in Counterinsurgency*, Santa Monica, Calif.: RAND Corporation, MG-1086-DOD, 2012. As of August 26, 2020: https://www.rand.org/pubs/monographs/MG1086.html

Connable, Ben, Michael J. McNerney, William Marcellino, Aaron Frank, Henry Hargrove, Marek N. Posard, S. Rebecca Zimmerman, Natasha Lander, Jasen J. Castillo, and James Sladden, *Will to Fight: Analyzing, Modeling, and Simulating the Will to Fight of Military Units*, Santa Monica, Calif.: RAND Corporation, RR-2341-A, 2018. As of August 26, 2020: https://www.rand.org/pubs/research_reports/RR2341.html

Cotton, Sarah K., Ulrich Petersohn, Molly Dunigan, Q Burkhart, Megan Zander-Cotugno, Edward O'Connell, and Michael Webber, *Hired Guns: Views About Armed Contractors in Operation Iraqi Freedom*, Santa Monica, Calif.: RAND Corporation, MG-987-SRF, 2010. As of August 26, 2020: https://www.rand.org/pubs/monographs/MG987.html

Defense One Radio, "Wagner and Russian Private Military Contractors," podcast episode, January 15, 2020. As of August 26, 2020: https://www.defenseone.com/ideas/2020/01/ep-62-wagner-and-russian-private-military-contractors/162447

DeGennaro, Patricia, "The Power of Cognitive Maneuver: Don't Underestimate Its Value," *Small Wars Journal*, September 19, 2017. As of August 26, 2020: https://smallwarsjournal.com/jrnl/art/the-power-of-cognitive-maneuver-don't-underestimate-its-value

Deiss, Joseph Jay, *Captains of Fortune: Profiles of Six Italian Condottieri*, New York: Thomas Y. Crowell Company, 1967.

Dunigan, Molly, *Victory for Hire: Private Security Companies' Impact on Military Effectiveness*, Palo Alto, Calif.: Stanford University Press, 2011.

Dunigan, Molly, Carrie M. Farmer, Rachel M. Burns, Alison Hawks, and Claude Messan Setodji, *Out of the Shadows: The Health and Well-Being of Private Contractors Working in Conflict Environments*, Santa Monica, Calif: RAND Corporation, RR-420-RC, 2013. As of August 26, 2020:
https://www.rand.org/pubs/research_reports/RR420.html

Elsea, Jennifer K., Moshe Schwartz, and Kennon H. Nakamura, *Private Security Contractors in Iraq: Background, Legal Status, and Other Issues*, Washington, D.C.: Congressional Research Service, RL32419, August 25, 2008.

Fainberg, Sarah, *Russian Spetsnaz: Contractors and Volunteers in the Syrian Conflict*, Paris: French Institute of International Relations, Russie.Nei.Visions, No. 105, December 2017. As of August 26, 2020:
https://www.ifri.org/en/publications/notes-de-lifri/russieneivisions/russian-spetsnaz-contractors-and-volunteers-syrian

Finch, Ray, "Private Russian Soldiers in Syria," *OE Watch*, Vol. 6, No. 10, October 2016, pp. 48–49.

Flanagan, Jane, "Mozambique Calls on Russian Firepower," *The Times*, October 2, 2019.

Giglio, Mike, "Inside the Shadow War Fought by Russian Mercenaries," BuzzFeed News, April 17, 2019. As of August 26, 2020:
https://www.buzzfeednews.com/article/mikegiglio/inside-wagner-mercenaries-russia-ukraine-syria-prighozhin

Goble, Paul A., "Russian Soldiers' Mothers Group Helping 7,000 Soldiers and Family Members Every Year," *Euromaidan Press*, October 4, 2014. As of August 26, 2020:
http://euromaidanpress.com/2014/10/04/russian-soldiers-mothers-group-helping-7000-soldiers-and-family-members-every-year

Gurcan, Metin, "Private Military Companies: Moscow's Other Army in Syria," Al-Monitor, November 30, 2017.

Hauer, Neil, "Putin Has a New Secret Weapon in Syria: Chechens," *Foreign Policy*, May 4, 2017.

Hawks, Alison, "I've Got Soul, but I'm Not a Soldier," *St. Antony's International Review*, Vol. 9, No. 2, February 2014, pp. 71–88.

Holt, William G. II, *Battlefield Contractors: Operational Risk and System Support Contractors*, Naval War College, Newport, R.I., October 27, 2010.

Institute of Medicine, *Returning Home from Iraq and Afghanistan: Assessment of Readjustment Needs of Veterans, Service Members, and Their Families*, Washington, D.C.: National Academies Press, 2013.

International Code of Conduct Association, "About Us," webpage, undated. As of December 22, 2020:
https://icoca.ch/about

International Committee of the Red Cross and Federal Department of Foreign Affairs of Switzerland, *The Montreux Document on Pertinent International Legal Obligations and Good Practices for States Related to Operations of Private Military and Security Companies During Armed Conflict*, Geneva, Switzerland, September 17, 2008. As of August 26, 2020: https://www.icrc.org/en/doc/assets/files/other/icrc_002_0996.pdf

Kelty, Ryan, "Citizen Soldiers and Civilian Contractors: Military Outsourcing, Unit Cohesion, and Retention Attitudes," Chestertown, Md.: Washington College, 2011.

Khazov-Cassia, Sergei, and Robert Coalson, "Russian Mercenaries: Vagner Commanders Describe Life Inside the 'Meat Grinder,'" Radio Free Europe/Radio Liberty, March 14, 2018. As of August 26, 2020: https://www.rferl.org/a/russian-mercenaries-vagner-commanders-syria/29100402.html

Klein, Margarete, *Private Military Companies: A Growing Instrument in Russia's Foreign and Security Policy Toolbox*, Helsinki, Finland: European Centre of Excellence for Countering Hybrid Threats, March 2019. As of August 26, 2020: https://www.hybridcoe.fi/wp-content/uploads/2019/06/HybridCoE_StrategicAnalysis_3_2019.pdf

Kopplin, Zack, and Irvin McCullough, "U.S. Paid $1B to Contractor Accused of Bigotry at Iraq Air Base," *Daily Beast*, September 18, 2018. As of August 26, 2020: https://www.thedailybeast.com/us-paid-dollar1b-to-contractor-accused-of-bigotry-at-iraq-air-base

Linder, Andrew, "Russian Private Military Companies in Syria and Beyond," *New Perspectives in Foreign Policy*, No. 16, Fall 2018, pp. 17–21. As of August 26, 2020: https://www.csis.org/npfp/russian-private-military-companies-syria-and-beyond

Lister, Tim, Sebastian Shukla, and Clarissa Ward, "Putin's Private Army," CNN, August 2019. As of August 26, 2020: https://edition.cnn.com/interactive/2019/08/africa/putins-private-army-car-intl

Lowell, Edward J., *The Hessians and the Other German Auxiliaries of Great Britain in the Revolutionary War*, New York: Harper and Brothers, 1884.

MacCoun, Robert J., "What Is Known About Unit Cohesion and Military Performance," in Bernard D. Rostker, Scott A. Harris, James P. Kahan, Erik J. Frinking, C. Neil Fulcher, Lawrence M. Hanser, Paul Koegel, John D. Winkler, Brent A. Boultinghouse, Joanna Heilbrunn, Janet Lever, Robert J. MacCoun, Peter Tiemeyer, Gail L. Zellman, Sandra H. Berry, Jennifer Hawes-Dawson, Samantha Ravich, Steven L. Schlossman, Timothy Haggarty, Tanjam Jacobson, Ancella Livers, Sherie Mershon, Andrew Cornell, Mark A. Schuster, David E. Kanouse, Raynard Kington, Mark Litwin, Conrad Peter Schmidt, Carl H. Builder, Peter Jacobson, Stephen A. Saltzburg, Roger Allen Brown, William Fedorochko, Marilyn Fisher Freemon, John F. Peterson, and James A. Dewer, *Sexual Orientation and U.S. Military Personnel Policy: Options and Assessment*, Santa Monica, Calif.: RAND Corporation, MR-323-OSD, 1993, pp. 283–331. As of August 26, 2020:
https://www.rand.org/pubs/monograph_reports/MR323.html

Machiavelli, Niccolò, *The Prince*, George Bull, trans., New York: Random House, 2003.

Mallett, Michael, *Mercenaries and Their Masters: Warfare in Renaissance Italy*, London: Bodley Head, 1974.

Marten, Kimberly, "Russia's Use of Semi-State Security Forces: The Case of the Wagner Group," *Post-Soviet Affairs*, Vol. 35, No. 3, 2019, pp. 181–204.

McCoy, Terrence, "What Does Russia Tell the Mothers of Soldiers Killed in Ukraine? Not Much," *Washington Post*, August 29, 2014.

Merriam-Webster, "Well-Being," *Merriam-Webster.com Dictionary*, undated. As of August 26, 2020:
https://www.merriam-webster.com/dictionary/well-being

Miller, T. Christian, "AIG Faces Inquiry over Medical Care for U.S. Contractors," ProPublica, April 22, 2009a. As of August 26, 2020:
http://www.propublica.org/article/
aig-faces-inquiry-over-medical-care-for-u.s.-contractors-422

———, "Congressional Hearing: Officials Admit Major Flaws in Program to Aid Wounded War-Zone Workers," ProPublica, June 19, 2009b. As of August 26, 2020:
http://www.propublica.org/article/
congressional-hearing-officials-acknowledge-program-to-treat-war-contra-619

———, "Foreign Workers for U.S. Are Casualties Twice Over," ProPublica, June 19, 2009c. As of August 26, 2020:
http://www.propublica.org/article/
foreign-workers-for-u.s.-are-casualties-twice-over-619

————, "The Other Victims of Battlefield Stress; Defense Contractors' Mental Health Neglected," ProPublica, February 26, 2010a. As of August 26, 2020: http://www.propublica.org/article/injured-contractors-the-other-victims-of-battlefield-stress-224

————, "This Year, Contractor Deaths Exceed Military Ones in Iraq and Afghanistan," ProPublica, September 23, 2010b. As of August 26, 2020: http://www.propublica.org/article/this-year-contractor-deaths-exceed-military-ones-in-iraq-and-afgh-100923

Miller, T. Christian, and Doug Smith, "Injured Civilians Battle to Get Care," *Los Angeles Times*, April 17, 2009.

Mockler, Anthony, *The Mercenaries*, New York: Macmillan, 1969.

Moore, Adam, *Empire's Labor: The Global Army That Supports U.S. Wars*, Ithaca, N.Y.: Cornell University Press, 2019.

Nelson, Kim M., *Contractors on the Battlefield: Force Multipliers or Force Dividers?* Maxwell Air Force Base, Ala.: Air Command and Staff College, April 2000.

Percy, Sarah, *Mercenaries: The History of a Norm in International Relations*, Oxford, UK: Oxford University Press, 2007.

Phinney, David, "Marines Jail Contractors in Iraq: Tension and Confusion Grow Amid the 'Fog of War,'" CorpWatch, June 7, 2005.

Prechtel, Johann Ernst, *A Hessian Officer's Diary of the American Revolution*, Bruce E. Burgoyne, trans., Bowie, Md.: Heritage Books, 1994.

Reynolds, Nathaniel, *Putin's Not-So-Secret Mercenaries: Patronage, Geopolitics, and the Wagner Group*, Washington, D.C.: Carnegie Endowment for International Peace, July 8, 2019. As of August 26, 2020: https://carnegieendowment.org/2019/07/08/putin-s-not-so-secret-mercenaries-patronage-geopolitics-and-wagner-group-pub-79442

Robinson, Linda, "America's Secret Armies: A Swarm of Private Contractors Bedevils the U.S. Military," *U.S. News and World Report*, November 4, 2002.

Robinson, Linda, Todd C. Helmus, Raphael S. Cohen, Alireza Nader, Andrew Radin, Madeline Magnuson, and Katya Migacheva, *Modern Political Warfare: Current Practices and Possible Responses*, Santa Monica, Calif.: RAND Corporation, RR-1772-A, 2018. As of August 26, 2020: https://www.rand.org/pubs/research_reports/RR1772.html

Rondeaux, Candace, *Decoding the Wagner Group: Analyzing the Role of Private Military Security Contractors in Russian Proxy Warfare*, Washington, D.C.: New America, November 7, 2019.

Rosengarten, Joseph George, *A Defence of the Hessians*, reprint, Philadelphia, Pa.: Historical Society of Pennsylvania, July 1899.

"Russia's Wagner Mercenaries Halt Prisoner Recruitment Campaign—Prigozhin," Reuters, February 9, 2023.

Schwartz, Moshe, and Joyprada Swain, *Department of Defense Contractors in Afghanistan and Iraq: Background and Analysis*, Washington, D.C.: Congressional Research Service, R40764, May 13, 2011.

Singer, P. W., *Corporate Warriors: The Rise of the Privatized Military Industry*, Ithaca, N.Y.: Cornell University Press, 2003.

Smith, Eugene B., "The New Condottieri and US Policy: The Privatization of Conflict and its Implications," *Parameters*, Vol. 32, No. 4, Winter 2002–2003, pp. 104–119.

Spearin, Christopher, "Special Operations Forces a Strategic Resource: Public and Private Divides," *Parameters*, Vol. 36, No. 4, Winter 2006–2007, pp. 58–70.

Sukhankin, Sergey, "War, Business and 'Hybrid' Warfare: The Case of the Wagner Private Military Company (Part Two)," *Eurasia Daily Monitor*, Vol. 15, No. 61, April 23, 2018a.

———, *"Continuing War by Other Means": The Case of Wagner, Russia's Premier Private Military Company in the Middle East*, Washington, D.C.: Jamestown Foundation, July 13, 2018b.

Swed, Ori, and Thomas Crosbie, "Who Are the Private Contractors in Iraq and Afghanistan?" *Military Times*, March 14, 2019. As of September 8, 2020: https://www.militarytimes.com/news/your-navy/2019/03/14/who-are-the-private-contractors-in-iraq-and-afghanistan

Thomson, Janice E., *Mercenaries, Pirates, and Sovereigns*, Princeton, N.J.: Princeton University Press, 1994.

Trading Economics, "Russia Average Monthly Wages," data for March 2020. As of September 8, 2020: https://tradingeconomics.com/russia/wages

Tsvetkova, Maria, "Russian Military Veterans Seek ICC Investigation of Mercenary Deployments," Reuters, November 9, 2018. As of August 26, 2020: https://www.reuters.com/article/us-russia-military-mercenaries/russian-military-veterans-seek-icc-investigation-of-mercenary-deployments-idUSKCN1NE2G7

Tsvetkova, Maria, and Anton Zverev, "Ghost Soldiers: The Russians Secretly Dying for the Kremlin in Syria," Reuters, November 3, 2016. As of August 26, 2020: https://www.reuters.com/article/us-mideast-crisis-syria-russia-insight/ghost-soldiers-the-russians-secretly-dying-for-the-kremlin-in-syria-idUSKBN12Y0M6

U.S. Army Special Operations Command, *Cognitive Maneuver for the Contemporary and Future Strategic Operating Environment*, May 31, 2016.

————, *Expanding Maneuver in the Early 21st Century Security Environment*, January 12, 2017. As of August 26, 2020:
https://www.soc.mil/Files/ExpandingManeuvers21Century.pdf

U.S. Army Sustainment Command, Public Affairs, "LOGCAP V Performance Contractors Selected," April 15, 2019. As of August 26, 2020:
https://www.army.mil/article/220353/logcap_v_performance_contractors_selected

U.S. Code, Title 10, Subtitle A, Chapter 3, Section 129a, General Policy for Total Force Management.

U.S. Department of Defense, *Summary of the 2018 National Defense Strategy of the United States of America: Sharpening the American Military's Competitive Edge*, January 19, 2018.

U.S. Department of Defense Instruction 1100.22, *Policy and Procedures for Determining Workforce Mix*, incorporating change 1, December 1, 2017.

U.S. General Accounting Office, *Military Operations: Contractors Provide Vital Services to Deployed Forces but Are Not Adequately Addressed in DoD Plans*, Washington, D.C., GAO-03-695, June 2003.

U.S. Special Operations Command, *Operating in the Human Domain*, version 1.0, August 3, 2015.

Waley, Daniel, The Italian City-Republics, London: World University Library, 1969.

Warburg, Robert A., U.S. Army Special Operations Command, "Cognitive Maneuver for the Contemporary and Future Strategic Operating Environment," briefing, June 21, 2016.

Weiss, Michael, "The Case of the Keystone Cossacks," *Foreign Policy*, November 21, 2013.

"What Is Russia's Wagner Group of Mercenaries and Why Did It March on Moscow?" BBC News, June 26, 2023.

Whitson, Anthony K., *Logistical Contractors on the Peacekeeping (PKO) Battlefield: A Guide for the Operational Commander*, Newport, R.I.: Naval War College, February 2001.

Zilber, Ariel, "Ex–Green Beret and Father-of-Four Who Worked as a Contractor for Lockheed Martin Dies After Being 'Pummeled into Unconsciousness by Two Marines During a Gym Altercation' While Working in Iraq," *Daily Mail*, January 8, 2019. As of August 26, 2020:
https://www.dailymail.co.uk/news/article-6567705/American-defense-contractor-Iraq-DIES-pummeled-unconsciousness-Marines.html

Zinn, Johann Georg, journal entry in Bruce E. Burgoyne, ed. and trans., *Enemy Views: The American Revolutionary War as Recorded by the Hessian Participants*, Westminster, Md.: Heritage Books, 1996.